Explore Barcelona

Guide   177

COVID-19

We have re-checked every business in this book before publication to ensure that it is still open after the COVID-19 outbreak. However, the economic and social impacts of COVID-19 will continue to be felt long after the outbreak has been contained, and many businesses, services and events referenced in this guide may experience ongoing restrictions. Some businesses may be temporarily closed, have changed their opening hours and services, or require bookings; some unfortunately could have closed permanently. We suggest you check with venues before visiting for the latest information.

Barcelona's
Top Experiences

Discover Gaudí's spectacular Sagrada Família
(p108)

ELOI_OMELLA/GETTY IMAGES ©

PIO3/SHUTTERSTOCK©

Admire the art and surrounds of Museu Picasso (p74)

BRIAN KINNEY/ALAMY STOCK PHOTO©

Check out the stunning architecture of La Pedrera (p112)

FUNDACIÓ JOAN MIRÓ, BARCELONA. FOTO: PEP HERRERO

See Miró's best at Fundació Joan Miró (p150)

Stare in wonder at Casa Batlló (p114)

Marvel at the magnificent Catedral (p42)

Step into Basílica de Santa Maria del Mar (p78)

Explore enchanting Park Güell (p132)

Take in the masterpieces of Museu Nacional d'Art de Catalunya (p148)

TAKASHI IMAGES/SHUTTERSTOCK ©

Stroll along La Rambla (p38)

PERESANZ/SHUTTERSTOCK ©

BORJA LARIA/SHUTTERSTOCK ©

Pick up a bargain at Mercat de la Boqueria (p44)

Catch an FC Barcelona game at Camp Nou (p168)

NATURSPORTS/SHUTTERSTOCK ©

Dining Out

Barcelona has a celebrated food scene fuelled by a combination of world-class chefs, superb markets and magnificent ingredients. Culinary masterminds such as Ferran and Albert Adrià, and Carles Abellán are reinventing the world of haute cuisine, while classic Catalan recipes and creative international flavours continue to earn accolades.

VOLANTHEVIST/GETTY IMAGES ©

New Catalan Cuisine

Avant-garde chefs have made Catalonia famous across the world for their food laboratories, their commitment to food as art and their mind-boggling riffs on the themes of traditional local cooking. Here the notion of gourmet cuisine is deconstructed as chefs transform liquids and solid foods into foams, create 'ice cream' of classic ingredients by means of liquid nitrogen, freeze-dry foods to make concentrated powders and employ spherification to create unusual and artful morsels. This alchemical cookery is known as molecular gastronomy, and invention is the keystone of this technique.

Classic Catalan Cuisine

Traditional Catalan recipes showcase the great produce of the Mediterranean: fish, prawns, cuttlefish, clams, pork, rabbit, game, first-rate olive oil, peppers, tomatoes, loads of garlic. Classic dishes also feature unusual pairings (seafood with meat, fruit with fowl) such as cuttlefish with chickpeas, cured ham with caviar, rabbit with prawns, or goose with pears.

Tapas

Tapas, those bite-sized morsels of joy, are not a typical Catalan concept, but tapas bars nonetheless abound all across Barcelona. Most open earlier than restaurants, making them a good pre-dinner (or instead-of-dinner) option. There are also plenty of wonderful Basque-style *pintxo* (pictured top right) bars dotted around.

©MAGDANATKA/SHUTTERSTOCK ©

Best Catalan

Can Recasens Superb local cooking, romantic Poblenou setting. (p100)

La Pubilla Lightly creative classics in Gràcia. (p138)

Cafè de l'Acadèmia High-quality dishes that never disappoint. (p51)

Cinc Sentits Jordi Artal's Michelin-star cuisine highlights Catalan produce. (p124)

Bar Muy Buenas Catalan faves amid 1920s decor. (p61)

Best Tapas

Quimet i Quimet Mouth-watering morsels served to a standing crowd. (p161)

Bar Pinotxo A legendary Boqueria joint. (p45)

Tapas 24 Everyone's favourite gourmet tapas bar. (p125)

Pepa Natural wines meet ambitious bites in L'Eixample. (p125)

Belmonte Hidden-away Barri Gòtic bodega with home-grown produce. (p52)

Best Gastronomy

Disfrutar Catalan cooking at its most experimental. (p122)

Enigma Travel through 40 avant-garde courses. (p161)

Lasarte The ultimate eating experience, with three Michelin stars. (p122)

La Barra de Carles Abellán Seafood presented in myriad creative ways. (p99)

Best Food Tours

Devour Barcelona Explore Barcelona's neighbourhoods through food. (p26)

Wanderbeak Small-group gastronomic jaunts. (p26)

Menú del Día

The *menú del dia*, a full set meal with water or wine, is a great way to cap prices at lunchtime. *Menús* start from around €11 and can go as high as €25. These days, all kinds of places offer a *menú*.

Barcelona on a Plate
Salsa Romesco

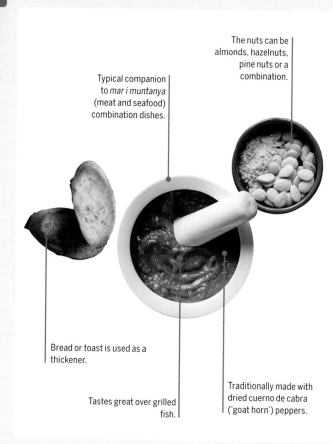

The nuts can be almonds, hazelnuts, pine nuts or a combination.

Typical companion to *mar i muntanya* (meat and seafood) combination dishes.

Bread or toast is used as a thickener.

Tastes great over grilled fish.

Traditionally made with dried cuerno de cabra ('goat horn') peppers.

★ Top Spots for Romesco

It's impossible not to stumble across a tasty romesco during your time in Barcelona. Most Catalan restaurants and plenty of creative newcomers have their own.

El 58 (p103) A French-Catalan Poblenou star for imaginative tapas.

Belmonte (p52) This tiny tapas spot in the Barri Gòtic whips up beautiful small plates.

Vivanda (p173) Magnificent Catalan cuisine showcasing seasonal fare.

Casa Delfín (p85) A culinary delight in El Born for Catalan–Mediterranean cooking.

A Catalan Classic

This classic Catalan sauce pervades the region's cuisine, popping up in numerous dishes as an accompaniment to roasted vegetables, grilled meats and fish. It's a rich, garlicky, nutty combination based on peppers and tomatoes. A thickened version, *salvitxada*, is the de rigueur dipping accompaniment for later-winter barbecues of *calçots*, those delicious leek-like onions beloved by Catalans.

Barbecued calcots and onions with *romesco* sauce

JULIA BOGDANOVA/SHUTTERSTOCK ©

NITO/SHUTTERSTOCK ©

Bar Open

Barcelona is a town for nightlife lovers, with an enticing spread of candlelit wine bars, old-school taverns, stylish lounges, magical cocktail hang-outs and kaleidoscopic nightclubs where the party continues until daybreak. For something a little more sedate, the city's atmospheric cafes and tea-houses make a fine retreat.

JONATHAN STOKES/LONELY PLANET ©

Bars & Lounges

Barcelona has a dizzying assortment of bars where you can start – or end – the night. Of course, where to go depends as much on the crowd as it does on ambience – and whether you're in the mood to drink at the latest hot spot (try Sant Antoni), with the bohemian crowd (El Raval) or among young expats (Gràcia and El Born).

Wine, Cava & Cocktail Bars

A growing number of wine bars scattered around the city showcase the great produce from Spain and beyond. A big part of the experience is sharing a few platters of cheese and charcuterie and plenty of tapas. Bars serving mostly or even exclusively natural, organic and/or biodynamic wines are surging in popularity. *Cava* bars tend to be more about the festive ambience than the actual drinking of *cava*, a sparkling white or rosé, most of which is produced in Catalonia's Penedès region. Barcelona's crafted-cocktail scene, meanwhile, has exploded in recent years.

Clubs

Barcelona's *discoteques* (*discotecas*; clubs) are at their best from Thursday to Saturday. A surprising variety of spots lurk in the old-town labyrinth; a sprinkling of well-known clubs is spread over L'Eixample and La Zona Alta. At the Port Olímpic, a strip of noisy waterfront clubs (such as Pacha, Opium, CDLC, Catwalk and Shôko) attracts raucous crowds of tourists, though at the time of writing it appeared these venues might close down.

ISTANBUL_IMAGE_VIDEO/SHUTTERSTOCK ©

Best for Wine Lovers

Perikete Lively wine and tapas bar in Barceloneta. (p103)

Viblioteca A trendy Gràcia space famed for its wine (and cheese) selections. (p143)

Bar Zim Pint-sized, cave-like Barri Gòtic bar showcasing lesser-known wines. (p54)

Can Paixano Perfect tapas pair with house rosé in La Barceloneta. (p95)

Best Cocktails

Paradiso Walk through a fridge to this glam speak-easy. (p88)

Dr Stravinsky The place to linger over an avant-garde concoction. (p81)

Two Schmucks Pop-up cocktail bar turned Raval sensation. (p68)

Bar Boadas An iconic drinking den going strong since the 1930s. (p55)

Best Dancing

La Terrrazza Party beneath palms in the Poble Espanyol. (p164)

Sala Apolo Gorgeous dance hall with varied electro, funk and more. (p155)

Moog Small Raval club that draws a fun, dance-loving crowd. (p69)

Beach Bars

During summer, small wooden beach bars, known as *xiringuitos* (*chiringuitos* in Spanish), open up along the sand from Barceloneta to Platja de la Nova Mar Bella, many with DJs and party vibes. We love **La Deliciosa** (www.panteabeach.com; Platja de Sant Miquel; ⏱9am-midnight Mar-Nov) and **Vai Moana** (www.panteabeach.com; Platja del Bogatell; ⏱9am-late Mar-Nov).

Barcelona in a Glass
Vermouth

Based on red or white wine, vermouth is infused with botanicals and fortified with brandy.

The perfect vermouth is usually served over ice and with an olive or two, and, sometimes, a slice of orange.

Vermouth is always accompanied by snacks, such as tapas of croquettes, anchovies, *patates braves* or even crisps

The hour of vermouth is as much about the intimate social scene as the drink itself.

Vermouth is thought to have arrived in Catalonia in the mid-19th century.

★ Best Places to Drink Vermouth

Quimet i Quimet (p161) House vermouth pairs with divine *montaditos* at this Poble Sec old-timer.

La Vermu (p143) Buzzy Gràcia favourite that makes its own vermouth.

La Vermuteria del Tano (p144) Gràcia's residents gather for traditional-style vermouth hour.

Bar Calders (p155) Lively Sant Antoni hub with perfect vermouth.

Bodega La Peninsular (p102) Barceloneta fave for homemade vermouth and superb tapas.

JOSE MONTORO/SHUTTERSTOCK ©

Salut!

Having become a favourite of Barcelona's working class in the run-up to the civil war, vermouth then fell out of favour (though certainly didn't disappear), but has experienced a dazzling revival over the last decade. New vermouth bars are opening all over town; historical vermouth joints are more popular than ever; and creative artisan varieties are on the up. Join the *barcelonins* for *la hora del vermut* (the hour of vermouth), typically around noon.

Vermouth with olives and potato chips

GARCIA FOTOGRAFÍA/SHUTTERSTOCK ©

Treasure Hunt

Barcelona's creative side is on show with its vibrant, understated shopping scene. The Ciutat Vella, L'Eixample and Gràcia host independent boutiques, historic shops, original stores, gourmet corners, designer labels and more; a raft of young creatives have set up boutiques and workshops in El Raval, El Born, Sant Antoni and Gràcia.

GILLES RIVEST/SHUTTERSTOCK ©

Boutique Barcelona

The heart of the Barri Gòtic has always been busy with small-scale merchants, but nowadays it's also the place for a more contemporary retail fix. Some of the most curious old shops, such as purveyors of hats, shoes and candles, lurk in the narrow lanes around Plaça de Sant Jaume. Once-seedy Carrer d'Avinyó has become a minor young-fashion boulevard. Antiques shops line Carrer de la Palla and Carrer dels Banys Nous. La Ribera is still home to a cornucopia of old-style specialist food and drink shops, but these days they're joined by stylish fashion boutiques, many of them with a sustainable ethos that champions local artisans and designers.

Vintage Fashion

El Raval is Barcelona's vintage fashion hot spot, where irresistible old-time stores mingle with a colourful array of affordable, mostly secondhand fashion boutiques. The central axis here is Carrer de la Riera Baixa, which plays host to '70s threads and military cast-offs. Carrer dels Tallers is also attracting a growing number of clothing and shoe shops (though music remains its core business). You'll also find a few vintage specialists in the Barri Gòtic, El Born and Sant Antoni.

Markets

Barcelona's food markets are some of the best in Europe; every neighbourhood has its own central market, and those in less touristed neighbourhoods are usually just as exciting as the traditional headliners.

MEINPHOTO/SHUTTERSTOCK ©

Best Fashion

Colmillo de Morsa Elegant women's designs in Gràcia. (p144)

La Manual Alpargatera Shop the Barri Gòtic for *espardenyes*. (p57)

Bagués-Masriera Exquisite jewellery from a company with a long tradition. (p117)

Ozz Barcelona Slow fashion and avant-garde Barcelona designers in El Born. (p91)

Avant Chic women's designer-wear. (p129)

Best Markets

Mercat de la Boqueria The quintessential Barcelona food market. (p44)

Mercat de Santa Caterina La Ribera's colourful alternative to La Boqueria. (p84; pictured above)

Mercat de Sant Antoni Beautifully restored neighbourhood market. (p158)

Mercat dels Encants Sprawling Poblenou flea market. (p105)

Best Food & Wine

Casa Gispert Roast nuts, chocolate, conserves and olive oils. (p91)

Vila Viniteca Cathedral of Spanish wines in El Born. (p90)

Caelum Deliciously wicked sweet treats made by nuns. (p54)

El Magnífico Barcelona's original coffee roastery, in El Born. (p90)

Antiques & Boutiques

Fashion and interior designers Lisa and Niki, at **Antiques & Boutiques** (☎ 671 234 800, 607 653 817; www.antiquesandboutiques.com; Plaça de la Mercè 8; Ⓜ Drassanes), run private, high-end fashion walking tours (from €300 for two) to help you get under the skin of Barcelona's creative design scene.

For Kids

Barcelona is great for older kids and teens – the Mediterranean attitude means they are included in many seemingly adult activities, such as eating late meals at bars or restaurants. Babies will love the welcoming Mediterranean culture, and toddlers will be showered with attention.

OLGA355/GETTY IMAGES ©

Dining Out with Kids

Barcelona – and Spain in general – is super-friendly when it comes to eating with children. Locals take their kids out all the time and don't worry too much about keeping them up late. Spanish kids tend to eat the Mediterranean offerings enjoyed by their parents, but many restaurants have children's menus that serve up burgers, pizzas, tomato-sauce pasta and the like; some places even have a kids' *menú del dia*. Good local – and childproof – options are *truita de patates/tortilla de patatas* (potato omelette), *pa amb tomàquet/pan con tomate* (bread rubbed with tomato and olive oil) and *croquetes/croquetas* (croquettes).

Practical Matters

○ Nappies (diapers), dummies, creams and formula can be bought at any of the city's many pharmacies and supermarkets. Nappies are cheaper in supermarkets.

○ Barcelona's metro is accessible and great for families with pushchairs. Be mindful of pickpockets.

○ The narrow streets of the Ciutat Vella, with their unpredictable traffic and cobbled streets, are less buggy-friendly than the rest of Barcelona.

○ Some restaurants and other venues have baby-changing tables, but certainly not all, and most places can rustle up a high chair. Many Spanish women breastfeed in public.

FRANTIC00/SHUTTERSTOCK ©

Best Attractions

Beaches Plenty of sand and gentle waters. (p25)

La Sagrada Família Gaudí's castle-like cathedral. (p108)

CosmoCaixa A fantastic science museum in the Zona Alta. (p171; pictured top right)

L'Aquàrium One of Europe's largest. (p98)

Poble Espanyol Travel through a mini-Spain. (p159)

Museu Picasso Older kids will love this outstanding museum in El Born. (p74)

Best Parks & Open Spaces

Parc de la Ciutadella Super-central park with a zoo, pond and playground. (p84)

Park Güell Glittering colours and *Hansel and Gretel*–like gatehouses. (p132)

Parc d'Atraccions Tibidabo A fabulous funfair with views. (p172)

Font Màgica This light show is guaranteed to make little ones shout 'Again!' (p158)

Parc Natural de Collserola A huge pine-sprinkled park in the northern hills. (p172)

Montjuïc Gardens, viewpoints and the fantastical Castell de Montjuïc. (p158)

Best Ways to See the City

By bike Barcelona has tonnes of bike tours and hire outlets. (p26)

By cable car Travel up Montjuïc from Barceloneta beach through the air. (p182; pictured top left)

Cuca de Llum New high-tech lightworm-like funicular to whisk you up Tibidabo. (p172)

Barcelona Time

Adjust your children to Barcelona time (ie late nights), otherwise they'll miss half of what's worth seeing. Local tourist offices can advise on activities.

Architecture

Barcelona is dotted with striking Gothic cathedrals, fantastical Modernista creations and avant-garde works. Building first boomed in the late Middle Ages, in the seat of the Catalan empire. In the late 19th century, the city was transformed through whimsical Modernisme. The third notable era of design began in the late 1980s and still continues. Get to grips with Barcelona's architecture on an expert-led guided tour (p26).

SOPOTNICKI/SHUTTERSTOCK ©

Best Gothic Giants

La Catedral The old city's Gothic centrepiece, at once extravagant and sombre. (p42)

Basílica de Santa Maria del Mar Arguably the high point of Catalan Gothic. (p78)

Basílica de Santa Maria del Pi A 14th-century jewel with a dazzling rose window. (p47)

Museu Marítim In the former Gothic shipyards just off the seaward end of La Rambla. (p98)

Reial Monestir de Santa Maria de Pedralbes A 14th-century monastery with a superb three-level cloister. (p171)

Museu Picasso Rare Gothic mansions, now converted artfully into exhibition space. (p74)

Best of Gaudí

La Sagrada Família Gaudí's unfinished symphony. (p108)

La Pedrera Showpiece Gaudí apartment building with an otherworldly roof. (p112)

Casa Batlló Eye-catching facade with an astonishing interior. (p114)

Palau Güell Gaudí's only building in the old part of town. (p63)

Park Güell The great architect's playfulness in full swing. (p132)

Best of the Modernista Rest

Palau de la Música Catalana Breathtaking concert hall by Lluís Domènech i Montaner. (p84; pictured)

Casa Amatller Josep Puig i Cadafalch's neighbour to Casa Batlló with gabled roof. (p120)

Casa Lleó Morera Domènech i Montaner's dancing nymphs, rooftop cupolas and interior stained glass. (p121)

Fundació Antoni Tàpies Brick and iron-framed masterpiece by Domènech i Montaner. (p120)

Recinte Modernista de Sant Pau Gilded pavilions by Domènech i Montaner. (p120)

Art & Design

For centuries Barcelona has been a canvas for artists – its streets, parks and galleries are littered with the signatures of artists past and present. From Modernista sculptors, such as Josep Llimona, to international stars like Roy Lichtenstein, they've all left their mark. Three of Spain's greatest 20th-century artists also have deep connections to Barcelona: Pablo Picasso, Joan Miró and Salvador Dalí.

SCULPTURE, L'ESTEL FERIT BY REBECCA HORN

EVGENIYA TELENNAYA/SHUTTERSTOCK ©

Best 20th-Century Art & Design

Museu Picasso A journey through Picasso's early work. (p74)

Fundació Joan Miró From formative years to later works. (p150)

Fundació Antoni Tàpies A selection of Tàpies' works and contemporary art exhibitions. (p120)

Museu Nacional d'Art de Catalunya Modern Catalan art at Barcelona's premier gallery. (p148)

MACBA Fabulous rotating collection of contemporary art. (p63)

Centre de Cultura Contemporània de Barcelona High-class rotating exhibitions, often focusing on photography. (p64)

CaixaForum Dynamic artistic space in a converted Modernista building. (p158)

Museu del Modernisme Barcelona Modernistas turn to home furnishings. (p122)

Best Street Art

L'Estel Ferit Rebecca Horn's tribute to Barceloneta's pre-Olympics waterfront culture. (p103; pictured)

Mosaïc de Miró The work of Barcelona's artistic icon adorns La Rambla. (p40)

Peix Frank Gehry's shimmering waterfront fish. (p103)

Gaudí's lamp posts One of Gaudí's earliest commissions, in the Barri Gòtic's Plaça Reial. (p47)

Articket BCN

Barcelona's best bargain for art lovers is the **Articket BCN** (www.articketbcn.org; €35), which gives you entry to six major galleries: MACBA, CCCB, Fundació Antoni Tàpies, Fundació Joan Miró, MNAC and Museu Picasso.

ESME FOX/LONELY PLANET ©

Museums & Galleries

Thanks to its rich heritage of art and architecture, Barcelona's array of world-class museums and galleries is unrivalled, from journeys into Catalan history to shimmering avant-garde sculpture stories. As always in Spain, the line between museum and art gallery is deliciously blurred; in classic Barcelona style, the wonderful buildings themselves are often a highlight.

Best History

Museu d'Història de Barcelona Rich Roman ruins and Gothic architecture. (p50)

Museu d'Història de Catalunya A wonderfully composed ode to Catalan history. (p98; pictured)

Museu Marítim Barcelona as Mediterranean port city in the Gothic former shipyards. (p98)

Camp Nou Experience Unravel the history of FC Barcelona. (p168)

Museu Etnològic Discover Catalan traditions and rituals. (p160)

MUHBA Refugi 307 Revisit wartime Barcelona in this evocative network of air-raid shelters. (p160)

Reial Monestir de Santa Maria de Pedralbes A window on monastic life and a marvellous Gothic cloister. (p171)

Museu d'Arqueologia de Catalunya Curious finds from across Catalonia and beyond. (p159)

Bunkers del Carmel Abandoned firing platforms with wrap-around views. (p138)

Best Art

Museu Nacional d'Art de Catalunya Breathtaking Romanesque art and a peerless portfolio of Catalan artists. (p148)

Museu Picasso The unmissable temple to Picasso's early genius. (p74)

Museu Frederic Marès Outstanding repository of Spanish sculpture, with Romanesque art the star. (p50)

Fundació Joan Miró Bold masterpieces in a soothing custom-designed gallery. (p150)

Fundació Antoni Tàpies Unravel the complex art of this 20th-century Catalan master. (p120)

MACBA Barcelona's greatest contemporary-art gallery. (p63)

Museu Gaudí Step inside Gaudí's mind and workshop with drawings and scale models. (p111)

Museu Can Framis (www.fundaciovilacasas.com) Learn about Catalan painting from the second half of the 20th century.

Parks & Beaches

IRENE MAJANO MAGANTO/GETTY IMAGES ©

The tight tangle of streets that consti-tutes Barcelona's old core can begin to feel claustrophobic, especially during high season. But once you move beyond, Barcelona opens up as a city washed with light, space and green: its parks, gardens and long stretches of golden sand lend an unmistakably Mediterranean air, and are more than worth seeking out.

Best Parks & Gardens

Park Güell Everybody's favourite public park, where zany Gaudí flourishes meet landscape gardening. (p132)

Parc de la Ciutadella Home to parliament, a zoo, public art and abundant shade. (p84)

Parc Natural de Collserola Wild, sprawling protected northern space, great for hiking, biking and running. (p172)

Jardins de Mossèn Cinto de Verdaguer Gentle, sloping Montjuïc gardens devoted to bulbs and water lilies. (p153)

Jardins de Laribal Alhambra-inspired gardens halfway up Montjuïc. (p153)

Parc del Laberint d'Horta An 18th-century north-Bar-celona delight centred on a meandering maze. (www.barcelona.cat; Passeig del Castanyers 1; pictured)

Best Beaches

El Poblenou Platges A string of lovely gold-sand beaches stretching north-east from the centre, includ-ing lively Bogatell and Nova Icària and LGBTIQ-friendly Mar Bella. (p98)

Platja de la Barceloneta Arrive early to savour this sunny old-timer without crowds. (p95)

Worth a Trip

Many of Barcelona's most gorgeous beaches lie outside the centre. Visit on a day trip, taking *rodalies* trains R1 or R2 from Plaça de Catalunya and Passeig de Gràcia respectively.

Platja de Castelldefels Around 20km southwest of central Barcelona; loved by kitesurfers.

Sitges Spain's most famous LGBTIQ+ holiday town, 35km southwest of Barcelona.

Platja del Garraf Tiny Garraf village, 30km southwest of Barcelona, trickles down to a sparkling teal bay.

Under the Radar

In recent years overtourism has unfortunately become a serious concern in Barcelona. By exploring beyond the busy tourist-driven pockets of town, you'll help build towards responsible tourism and a sustainable local environment, while also uncovering everything from delightful neighbourhood restaurants to architectural jewels in the far-flung corners of this fabulous city.

INFINITI777/SHUTTERSTOCK ©

Outer Neighbourhoods

Staying in less touristed, outer Barcelona *barris* gives you the chance to tap into local life, support small neighbourhood businesses, explore quieter sights and gain a broader perspective of the city. Smart Sarrià-Sant Gervasi in northwest Barcelona, peaceful northern Horta (with its garden labyrinth) and the Sants/Les Corts area west of the centre make excellent bases.

Fun Alternatives

Parc Natural de Collserola Hike and bike the vast green expanses. (p172)

Beaches Head to beaches further out of town. (p25)

Pedralbes Explore a 14th-century convent. (pictured above; p171)

El Poblenou Check out this area bursting with creative projects. (p98)

Poble Sec Tap into buzzy tapas bars and sloping streets. (p154)

Specialised Tours

A wonderful way to really get to know Barcelona is to tour it with a local expert.

Devour Barcelona (www. devourbarcelonafoodtours. com; tours €79-119) Neighbourhood-focused food tours.

Wanderbeak (www.wanderbeak.com; group tour per person €79-99) Small-group gastronomic experiences.

Barcelona Architecture Walks (www.barcelonarchitecturewalks.com; 3hr tour €38) Design-led itineraries with local architects.

Barcelona Street Style Tour (www.barcelonastreetstyletour.com; by donation) Donation-based street-art tours.

Runner Bean Tours (www.runnerbeantours.com; by donation) Thematic pay-what-you-wish tours.

LGBTIQ+ Barcelona

Barcelona has a vibrant LGBTIQ+ scene, with a lively array of bars, clubs, restaurants and even specialised bookshops in the 'Gaixample', an area of L'Eixample about five to six blocks southwest of Passeig de Gràcia around Carrer del Consell de Cent. Other LGBTIQ-focused venues are dotted around Sant Antoni and Poble Sec.

NITO/SHUTTERSTOCK ©

Best Bars

La Monroe (Map p62, C4; ☎93 441 94 61; www.lamonroe.es; Plaça Salvador Seguí 1-9; ☺noon-late; 🛜; MLiceu) Stylish, low-key, all-welcoming bar in El Raval's Filmoteca.

La Chapelle (☎93 453 30 76; Carrer de Muntaner 67; ☺4pm-2am Sun-Thu, to 2.30am Fri & Sat; MUniversitat) Casual Gaixample spot for cocktails.

La Federica (☎93 600 59 01; www.facebook.com/barlafederica; Carrer de Salvà 3; ☺7pm-1am Tue, to 2am Wed & Thu, to 3am Fri & Sat; MParal·lel) Tasty wines, tapas and cocktails in Poble Sec, plus events.

Best Parties

Arena Madre (☎93 487 83 42; www.grupoarena.com; Carrer de Balmes 32; €10-12; ☺12.30am-5am Sun-Thu, to 6am Fri & Sat; MPasseig de Gràcia) With striptease shows and pumping beats.

Arena Classic (☎93 487 83 42; www.grupoarena.com; Carrer de la Diputació 233; €6-12; ☺11pm-3am Thu, to 6am Fri & Sat; MPasseig de Gràcia) Buzzing LGBTIQ+ club with plenty of lesbian events.

Pride Barcelona (www.pridebarcelona.org; ☺late Jun-early Jul; pictured) Two weeks in summer.

Hedonistic Sitges

Spain's LGBTIQ+ capital is hedonistic Sitges. This attractive town hosts some fabulous LGBTIQ-oriented beaches, a raucous Carnaval in February/March, and a Pride march in June.

Four Perfect Days

Day 1

Head out early to explore the Barri Gòtic. Peek inside **La Catedral** (p42) and stroll through Plaça de Sant Josep Oriol, Plaça Reial and Plaça Sant Just, before visiting the **Museu d'Història de Barcelona** (p50). **La Rambla** (p38) and the **Mercat de la Boqueria** (p44) are peaceful early in the day. Lunch at **Cafè de l'Acadèmia** (p51).

Wander over to El Born, which is packed with treasures: the **Basílica de Santa Maria del Mar** (p78), **Carrer de Montcada** (p86), the **Museu Picasso** (p74) Swing by the **Palau de la Música Catalana** (p84; pictured) or the **Mercat de Santa Caterina** (p84).

Don't miss the tapas and *cava* (sparkling wine) at **Bar del Pla** (p81) and **El Xampanyet** (p81). End at **Bar Sauvage** (p81) or **Farola** (p81).

Day 2

Start with **La Sagrada Família** (p108), Gaudí's wondrous work in progress, where you've (hopefully) prebooked a guided tour. Also visit the lesser-known **Recinte Modernista de Sant Pau** (p120; pictured), by Domènech i Montaner. For lunch, hit buzzy **Passeig de Sant Joan** (p124) or **Tapas 24** (p125).

Explore more great Modernisme along **Passeig de Gràcia**, including Gaudí's houses – **Casa Batlló** (p114) and **La Pedrera** (p112) – again, prebooking helps! If time and energy allow, L'Eixample is full of fabulous shopping.

Zip up to village-like Gràcia and wander through its enchanting streets. Grab a vermouth at **La Vermu** (p143), wines at **Vibli-oteca** (p143) and/or Catalan cooking at **La Pubilla** (p138).

Day 3

SCULPTURE, EL PEIX BY FRANK GEHRY, SPATULETAIL/SHUTTERSTOCK ©

Time to take in the Mediterranean along the **Passeig Marítim** (p95; pictured). Then wander through Barceloneta, stopping at the **Mercat de la Barceloneta** (p95), before early tapas at **La Cova Fumada** (p95).

Afterwards, peel back the centuries at the **Museu d'Història de Catalunya** (p98) or relax at the beach – the **El Poblenou beaches** (p98) are less touristed.

After freshening up, make your way over to up-and-coming El Poblenou for dinner at candlelit **Can Recasens** (p100). Meander along **Rambla del Poblenou** (p99) and its surrounding streets, where creative spots like **Espai Joliu** (p103) showcase the area's regeneration. Check out bars like **Madame George** (p104) or **Balius** (p104).

Day 4

DAN COVEY/LONELY PLANET ©

Kick things off with a scenic cable-car ride up to Montjuïc, followed by a stroll to the **Museu Nacional d'Art de Catalunya** (p148), perhaps via the terrace cafe at **Salts Montjuïc** (p153).

Then wander through the sloping neighbourhood of Poble Sec, where **Palo Cortao** (p162) and **Quimet i Quimet** (p161) are foodie favourites. Hop across Avinguda del Paral·lel to trendyfied Sant Antoni, checking out the wonderful **Mercat de Sant Antoni** (p158; pictured) and **Carrer del Parlament**.

Spend the evening soaking up bohemian El Raval. See an exhibition at the **MACBA** (p63) or an indie feature at the **Filmoteca de Catalunya** (p69). Finish with dinner at **Elisabets** (p61) and bar-hop along **Carrer de Joaquín Costa**.

Need to Know

For detailed information, see Survival Guide (p177)

Population
1.62 million

Currency
Euro (€)

Language
Spanish, Catalan

Visas
EU & Schengen countries No visa required.
UK, Australia, Canada, Israel, Japan, NZ & the US ETIAS pre-authorisation to be introduced in 2022.
Other countries Check with local Spanish embassy.

Money
ATMs are widely available. Credit cards are widely accepted.

Mobile Phones
Local SIM cards can generally be used in unlocked European, Australian and North American phones.

Time
Central European Time (GMT/UTC plus one hour)

Daily Budget

Budget: Less than €60
Dorm bed: €15–40
Set lunch: from €12
Bicycle hire per hour: €5
Tapas: €2 to €4 per tapa

Midrange: €60–200
Standard double room: €80–170
Two-course dinner with wine: from €25
Guided tours and museum tickets: €15–40

Top end: More than €200
Double room in boutique and luxury hotels: from €200
Three-course meal at top restaurants: €80
Concert tickets to Palau de la Música Catalana: around €45

Useful Websites

Barcelona (www.barcelona.cat) Town hall's official site, with plenty of links.

Barcelona Turisme (www.barcelonaturisme.com) City's official tourism website.

Lonely Planet (www.lonelyplanet.com/barcelona) Destination information, hotel reviews and more.

Spotted by Locals (www.spottedbylocals.com/barcelona) Insider tips.

Miniguide (https://miniguide.co) Style-conscious reviews and advice from locals.

Time Out Barcelona (www.timeout.com/barcelona) Great for restaurants and nightlife.

Foodie in Barcelona (www.foodieinbarcelona) Fab Barcelona food blog.

Arriving in Barcelona

✈ Aeroport de Barcelona–El Prat

Frequent *aerobuses* into town (€5.90, 35 minutes) from 5.35am to 1.05am. Taxis cost €25 to €35. Train and metro also handy.

🚉 Estació Sants

Long-distance trains arrive at this large station near the centre of town, which is linked by metro to other parts of the city. Some international buses arrive into the adjacent Estació d'Autobusos de Sants.

🚉 Estació d'Autobusos Barcelona Nord

Barcelona's main long-haul bus station is 1.5km northeast of Plaça de Catalunya, near the Arc de Triomf metro station in L'Eixample.

✈ Aeroport Girona–Costa Brava

Direct buses to/from Barcelona's Estació del Nord bus station (€16, 1¼ hours).

✈ Aeroport de Reus

Buses run to/from the Estació d'Autobusos de Sants (€16, 1¾ hours).

Getting Around

The excellent metro can get you most places, with buses and trams filling in the gaps. Single-ride tickets on all standard transport within Zone 1 cost €2.40; the 10-ride Targeta Casual costs €11.35. Taxis are best late at night.

Ⓜ Metro

Runs 5am to midnight Sunday to Thursday, to 2am Friday and 24 hours on Saturday.

🚌 Bus

Buses run along most city routes every few minutes from around 5am to around 11pm.

🚕 Taxi

Taxis are easily flagged down, or booked online or by phone or app.

🚲 Bicycle

Barcelona has over 180km of bike lanes and numerous bike-hire outlets.

🚠 Cable Car

Two cable cars zip up Montjuïc hill.

Barcelona Neighbourhoods

Gràcia & Park Güell (p131)
To the north of laid-back, village-like Gràcia lies one of Gaudí's most captivating works.

Park Güell

La Sagrada Família

La Pedrera

Casa Batlló

Museu Picasso

La Catedral

Camp Nou & Barça Stadium Tour

La Rambla

Mercat de la Boqueria

Basílica de Santa Maria del Mar

Museu Nacional d'Art de Catalunya (MNAC)

Fundació Joan Miró

Camp Nou, Pedralbes & La Zona Alta (p167)
Home to FC Barcelona, a serene 14th-century monastery, Tibidabo and its pine-sprinkled slopes, and lovely Sarrià.

Montjuïc, Poble Sec & Sant Antoni (p147)
Montjuïc hosts wonderful museums, a formidable castle and scented gardens, while Poble Sec and Sant Antoni are trendy havens.

La Ribera & El Born (p73)

Splendid architecture, original boutiques and fabulous tapas and cocktail bars await alongside a standout neighbourhood market and the Museu Picasso.

La Rambla & Barri Gòtic (p37)

The old heart of Barcelona is a vision of medieval streets, monumental buildings, city bustle and the famous Mercat de la Boqueria.

Barceloneta, the Waterfront & El Poblenou (p93)

Wander the traditional fishing quarter of Barceloneta, the sparkling beaches and the up-and-coming neighbourhood of El Poblenou.

El Raval (p59)

Barcelona's most multicultural *barri* is a fascinating jumble of ambitious art galleries, busy bars and restaurants, and an unlikely Gaudí confection.

La Sagrada Família & L'Eixample (p107)

Explore Modernista treasures, broad boulevards, outstanding bars and restaurants and a shopping paradise.

Explore
Barcelona

Barcelona's Walking Tours 🚶🚶

Human tower at Festa Major de Gràcia (p144) SERGI ESCRIBANO/GETTY IMAGES©

Explore

La Rambla & Barri Gòtic

La Rambla, Barcelona's most famous pedestrian boulevard, is always a hive of activity, busy with tourists, locals and con artists (watch out!). The adjoining Barri Gòtic is packed with historical treasures – relics of ancient Rome, 14th-century Gothic churches and atmospheric cobblestone lanes lined with shops, bars and restaurants.

The Short List

○ **La Catedral (p42)** Exploring the spectacular cloister and shadowy chapels of this Gothic masterpiece, before visiting Barcelona's ancient Call (Jewish quarter).

○ **Museu d'Història de Barcelona (p50)** Strolling through the subterranean ruins of Roman Barcino.

○ **Mercat de la Boqueria (p44)** Feasting on tapas and weaving between fresh-produce stalls – early on!

○ **Museu Frederic Marès (p50)** Wandering through the strange and wondrous collections of a rich Catalan artist.

○ **La Rambla (p38)** Rising early to take in Barcelona's liveliest street scene, with its flower stalls, historical sights and saunterers from every corner of the globe.

Getting There & Around

Ⓜ Key stops include Catalunya, Liceu, Drassanes, Jaume I and Urquinaona.

🚌 Airport and night buses arrive and depart from Plaça de Catalunya.

🚗 Easiest to catch on La Rambla or Plaça de Catalunya.

Neighbourhood Map on p48

Carrer de Montjuïc del Bisbe, Barri Gòtic (p46) DAVID J. LEW/500PX ©

Top Experience
Stroll along La Rambla

Barcelona's most famous street is both a tourist magnet (beware the pickpockets and con artists) and a window into Catalan culture. Flanked by plane trees, the middle of La Rambla is a broad pedestrian boulevard, always crowded with a wide cross-section of society. Though the busy tourist-centric scene won't appeal to everyone, a stroll here is pure sensory overload: churches, theatres and intriguing architecture mingle with souvenir hawkers and pavement artists.

◉ MAP P48, C6

Ⓜ Catalunya, Liceu, Drassanes

History

La Rambla takes its name from a seasonal stream (*ramal* in Arabic) that once ran here. From the early Middle Ages, it was better known as the Cagalell (Stream of Shit) and lay outside the city walls until the 14th century. Monastic buildings were then built (many were later destroyed) and, subsequently, mansions of the well-to-do from the 16th to the early 19th centuries. Unofficially, La Rambla is divided into five sections, which explains why many know it as Las Ramblas (Les Rambles in Catalan).

Horrific terrorist attacks in 2017, which killed 14 people, did little to diminish La Rambla's popularity with visitors or with the many hawkers, performers and living statues.

La Rambla de Canaletes

The initial stretch south from Plaça de Catalunya is named after the **Font de Canaletes** (La Rambla; Ⓜ Catalunya), an inconspicuous turn-of-the-20th-century drinking fountain and lamp post. Delirious football fans gather here to celebrate whenever the main home side, FC Barcelona, wins a cup or the league championship.

La Rambla dels Estudis

Running south from Carrer de la Canuda to Carrer de la Portaferrissa, La Rambla dels Estudis is named for the 15th-century university that once stood here.

Església de Betlem

Where La Rambla meets Carrer del Carme, this **church** (Ⓙ 93 318 38 23; www.mdbetlem.net; Carrer d'en Xuclà 2; ◷ 8.30am-1.30pm & 6-9pm; Ⓜ Liceu) was constructed in baroque style for the Jesuits in the late 17th and early 18th centuries to replace a 15th-century church destroyed by fire in 1671. Anarchists torched it again in 1936.

★ Top Tips

o La Rambla is at its best first thing in the morning, before the cruise ship crowds arrive.

o Keep an eye on your belongings and wear backpacks on your front. Pickpockets find easy pickings along this stretch.

✕ Take a Break

For a proper sit-down meal, your best nearby bet is at one of the many restaurants ringing the Plaça Reial (p47), or try Elisabets (p61) just into El Raval.

Grab a coffee at **Café de l'Òpera** (Ⓙ 93 317 75 85; www.cafeoperabcn.com; La Rambla 74; ◷ 8.30am-2.30am; 🛜; Ⓜ Liceu) or dip into El Raval for a more cutting-edge caffeine scene at Bar Central (p65).

Palau Moja

Looming over the eastern side of La Rambla, the neoclassical **Palau Moja** (www.palaumoja.com; Carrer de Portaferrissa 1; admission free; ⏱10am-9pm; Ⓜ Liceu) dates from the second half of the 18th century. These days it houses a centre for Catalan heritage and a well-stocked tourist office.

La Rambla de Sant Josep

From Carrer de la Portaferrissa to Plaça de la Boqueria, what is officially called La Rambla de Sant Josep (named after a now nonexistent monastery) is lined with flower stalls, which give it the popular alternative name La Rambla de les Flors. It's flanked on the west side by the buzzing Mercat de la Boqueria (p44).

Palau de la Virreina

A rare example of post-baroque architecture in Barcelona, the **Palau de la Virreina** (📞93 316 10 00; https://ajuntament.barcelona.cat; La Rambla 99; admission free; ⏱11am-8pm Tue-Sun; Ⓜ Liceu) is a grand 18th-century rococo mansion (with some neoclassical elements) that now hosts rotating photography exhibitions.

Mosaïc de Miró & Memorial

At Plaça de la Boqueria, you can walk all over a colourful 1976 pavement **mosaic** (Ⓜ Liceu), with one tile signed by the artist, Miró, who was born nearby on Passatge del Crèdit. Right next to the mosaic, a 12m-long engraved **memorial** commemorates the 14 victims of the 2017 terrorist

Casa Quadros on La Rambla

van attack on La Rambla, with an anti-violence message inscribed in multiple languages.

Casa de Bruno Cuadros

Remodelled by Josep Vilaseca in 1883, the former Casa dels Paraigües (House of the Umbrellas) **shop** (La Rambla 82; M Liceu) prominently advertised its wares with wall-mounted cast-iron parasols, Egyptian imagery and an ornate Chinese dragon.

Escribà

Chocolates, dainty pastries and mouth-watering cakes await behind a Modernista mosaic facade at beloved Barcelona bakery **Escribà** (93 301 60 27; www. escriba.es; La Rambla 83; ⏰9am-9pm; 📶; M Liceu), owned by the Escribà family, a name synonymous with sinfully good sweet things. More than that, it adds a touch of authenticity to La Rambla.

La Rambla dels Caputxins

La Rambla dels Caputxins, named after a former monastery, runs from Plaça de la Boqueria to Carrer dels Escudellers. The latter is named for the potters' guild, founded in the 13th century. On the western side of La Rambla is

Escaping the Crowds

As one of the most touristed spots in Barcelona, there's no denying that La Rambla can feel a bit like a packed-out circus. Swing by first thing, around 8am, to enjoy this historic leafy boulevard with far fewer crowds. Alternatively, you could seek out some of the city's quieter *rambles* instead, such as Rambla del Raval (p65) or Rambla del Poblenou (p99).

the Gran Teatre del Liceu (p55); to the southeast is the palm-shaded Plaça Reial (p47). Below this point La Rambla gets seedier.

La Rambla de Santa Mónica

The final stretch of La Rambla widens out to approach the Mirador de Colom overlooking Port Vell. La Rambla here is named after the Convent de Santa Mònica, now the **Centre d'Art Santa Mònica** (93 316 28 10; http://artssantamonica. gencat.cat; La Rambla 7; admission free; ⏰11am-9pm Tue-Sat, to 7pm Sun Apr-Oct, 10am-8pm Tue-Sat, to 7pm Sun Nov-Mar; M Drassanes).

Top Experience 📷

Marvel at the magnificent Catedral

Barcelona's central place of worship presents a magnificent image. The richly decorated main facade, dotted with gargoyles and the kinds of stone intricacies you would expect of northern European Gothic, sets it quite apart from other Barcelona churches. The facade was actually added from 1887 to 1890. The rest of the building dates between 1298 and 1460.

◉ MAP P48, D3

www.catedralbcn.org

Plaça de la Seu

€7, roof or choir €3, chapter house €2

🕑 tourist visits 12.30-7.45pm Mon-Fri, 12.30-5.30pm Sat, 2-5.30pm Sun

Ⓜ Jaume I

The Interior & Roof

The interior is a broad, soaring space divided into a central nave and two aisles by lines of elegant, slim pillars. The cathedral was one of the few churches in Barcelona spared by the anarchists in the civil war, so its ornamentation, never overly lavish, is intact. In the middle of the central nave is the exquisitely sculpted late-14th-century timber *coro* (choir stalls; €3; closed during worshipping hours). A broad staircase before the main altar leads down to the crypt, which contains the 14th-century tomb of Santa Eulàlia, one of Barcelona's two patron saints.

Apart from the cathedral's main facade, the rest is sparse in decoration, and the octagonal, flat-roofed towers are a clear reminder that, even here, Catalan Gothic architectural principles prevailed. For a bird's-eye view, visit the roof and tower by taking the lift (€3) from the Capella dels Sants Innocents.

Claustre

From the southwest transept, exit by the partly Romanesque door next to the coffins of Count Ramon Berenguer I and his wife Almodis, founders of the original Romanesque church. You'll then enter the leafy *claustre* (cloister), with its tinkling fountains and flock of 13 geese. The geese supposedly represent the age of Santa Eulàlia at the time of her martyrdom and have, generation after generation, been squawking here since medieval days. The **Capella de Santa Llúcia** is another of the few reminders of Romanesque Barcelona (although the interior is largely Gothic).

Casa de l'Ardiaca

Opposite the cathedral, the 16th-century **Casa de l'Ardiaca** (Arxiu Històric; ☑93 256 22 55; https://ajuntament.barcelona.cat; Carrer de Santa Llúcia 1; admission free; ⊙9am-7.30 Mon-Fri, 10am-7.30pm Sat; Ⓜ Jaume I) has housed the city's archives since the 1920s and was renovated by Lluís Domènech i Montaner in 1902.

★ Top Tips

o It is worth paying for the 'donation entrance' to avoid the crowds and appreciate the splendour of the building in relative peace.

o If you're around at 6pm Saturday or 11am Sunday, check out the *sardanes* (the Catalan national dance) performed in the square in front of the cathedral.

✕ Take a Break

Head to Placeta de Manuel Ribé in the old Jewish quarter, where Salterio (p54) serves fragrant fresh mint tea and Levante (p53) does delectable Mediterranean–Middle Eastern cuisine.

Or find steaming churros at **Xurreria** (☑93 318 76 91; Carrer dels Banys Nous 8; cone €1-2; ⊙7am-1.30pm & 3.30-8.15pm Mon, Tue, Thu & Fri, 7am-2pm & 4-8.30pm Sat, 7am-2.30pm & 4.30-8.30pm Sun; Ⓜ Liceu).

Top Experience 📷
Pick up a bargain at Mercat de la Boqueria

Barcelona's most central fresh-produce market is one of Europe's greatest sound, smell and colour sensations – housed in an impressive Modernista-influenced building on the site of the former Sant Josep monastery. It may have taken a touristy turn of late, but towards the back you'll touch upon its soul: bountiful culinary delights.

◎ **MAP P48, B4**

📞 93 318 20 17

www.boqueria.barcelona

La Rambla 91

🕑 8am-8.30pm Mon-Sat

Ⓜ Liceu

History

There is believed to have been a market on this spot since 1217, and as much as La Boqueria has become a modern-day attraction, some *barcelonins* do still try to shop here (usually early on). What is now known as La Boqueria didn't come to exist until the 19th century. The iron Modernista gate was added in 1914.

Catalan Specialities

Many of Barcelona's top restaurateurs also come here for their produce, though nowadays it's no easy task getting through the crowds to that slippery slab of sole or tempting piece of Asturian goat's cheese.

Whether you eat here or self-cater, don't miss the chance to try some of Catalonia's gastronomical specialities, such as *bacallà salat* (dried salted cod), *calçots* (a cross between a leek and an onion), *cargols* (snails), *peus de porc* (pig's trotters) or *percebes* (goose barnacles). La Boqueria is dotted with a handful of vibrant, unassuming places to eat, many with charismatic owners at the helm.

Seafood & Charcuterie

Though these days tourist-enticing fruit-shake stalls and novelty chocolates abound, the fish market in La Boqueria's geographical centre is the guardian of tradition. Razor clams and red prawns, salmon, sea bass and swordfish, all almost as fresh as when it was caught.

Among the many piled-high stalls, don't miss family-owned **Joan La Llar del Pernil** (📞93 317 95 29; www.joanlallardelpernil.com; Stalls 667-671; ⏱8am-3pm Tue-Thu, to 7pm Mon & Fri, 7.30am-4pm Sat), which sells some of the best *pernil* (cured Spanish-style ham; *jamón* in Castilian) and charcuterie in the city. The specialty is *jamón ibérico de bellota*, sourced from free-roaming acorn-fed pigs.

★ Top Tips

○ • La Boqueria has become extremely overcrowded in recent years. Go early. Or for a more tranquil market experience, consider the Mercat de Sant Antoni (p158) or Mercat de Santa Caterina (p84) instead.

○ • Many stalls, including most fish stalls, are closed on Monday.

○ • Ask permission before taking stallholders' pictures, and buy something if you do.

✗ Take a Break

For some of La Boqueria's best cooking, visit **El Quim** (📞93 301 98 10; www.elquimdelaboqueria.com; tapas €3-5, mains €10-26; ⏱noon-4pm Mon & Wed, 8am-4pm Tue & Thu, 8am-5pm Fri & Sat).

To soak up the clamour from a front-row vantage point, stop by **Bar Pinotxo** (📞93 317 17 31; www.pinotxobar.com; tapas €4-16; ⏱6.30am-4pm Mon-Sat).

Walking Tour 🥾

Hidden Historical Treasures of the Barri Gòtic

This scenic walk through the Barri Gòtic will take you back in time, from the early days of Roman-era Barcino through to the medieval era. The 20th century has also left its mark here, from artistic contributions to the tragic scars of the Spanish Civil War.

Walk Facts

Start Col·legi d'Arquitectes; Ⓜ Jaume I

End Plaça del Rei; Ⓜ Jaume I

Length 1.5km; two hours

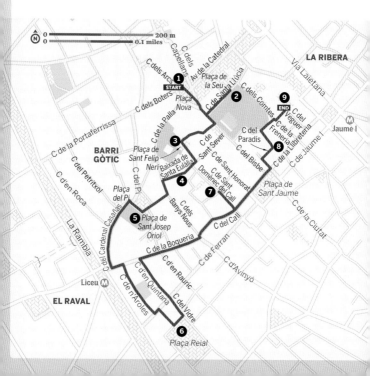

❶ Picasso

Start by admiring the facade of the 1931 **Col·legi de Arquitectes** (https://arquitectes.cat; Plaça Nova; **P**; **M** Jaume I) facing the Plaça Nova. This giant 1962 contribution by Picasso represents Mediterranean festivals.

❷ La Catedral

Wander through **La Catedral** (p42), one of the few churches in Barcelona spared by the anarchists in the civil war. Don't miss the cloister with its flock of 13 geese.

❸ Plaça de Sant Felip Neri

Leave the cathedral from the cloister and turn right, then turn left down narrow Carrer de Montjuïc del Bisbe into **Plaça de Sant Felip Neri** (**M** Jaume I, Liceu), damaged by pro-Francoist bombers in 1938; a plaque commemorates the victims (mostly children).

❹ Santa Eulàlia

Head south out on to Baixada de Santa Eulàlia and turn right. On this slender lane, you'll spot a small **statue of Santa Eulàlia**, one of Barcelona's patron saints who suffered various tortures during her martyrdom.

❺ Basílica de Santa Maria del Pi

Make your way west to the looming 14th-century **Basílica de Santa Maria del Pi** (93 318 47 43; www.basilicadelpi.cat; Plaça del Pi; adult/concession/child under 8yr €4.50/3.50/free; 10am-6pm; **M** Liceu), famed for its magnificent rose window.

❻ Plaça Reial

Follow the curving road and zigzag down to **Plaça Reial** (**M** Liceu), one of Barcelona's prettiest squares. Flanking the fountain are lamp posts designed by Antoni Gaudí.

❼ Sinagoga Major

Stroll north to Carrer de la Boqueria and turn left on Carrer de Salomó Ben Adret. This leads into El Call, once the heart of Barcelona's Jewish quarter, until the bloody pogrom of 1391. The **Sinagoga Major** (p50), one of Europe's oldest, was discovered in 1996.

❽ Roman Temple

Head across Plaça de Sant Jaume and turn left on Carrer del Paradís. You'll soon pass the unassuming entrance to the **Temple d'August** (93 256 21 22; www.muhba.cat; Carrer del Paradís 10; admission free; 10am-2pm Mon, to 7pm Tue-Sat, to 8pm Sun; **M** Jaume I): four Roman columns in a small courtyard.

❾ Plaça del Rei

Your final stop is grand **Plaça del Rei** (**M** Jaume I), where the Reyes Católicos (Catholic Monarchs) received Columbus following his first voyage to the Americas. The former palace today houses the superb **Museu d'Història de Barcelona** (p50).

La Rambla & Barri Gòtic

A
B
C
D
E
F

1
2
3
4

Plaça de Catalunya

Plaça de Ramon Amadeu

C de Santanna

C de Bertrellans

Av del Portal de l'Àngel

Plaça de la Vila de Madrid

C de la Canuda

C de C la Canuda

C Comtal

Ptge del Patriarca

Els Quatre Gats

C de Montsió

C de n'Amargós

C de les Magdalenes

C de Duran i Bas

C de Ripoll

C dels Capellans

C dels Sagristans

Via Laietana

C del Dr Joaquim Pou

9 ✗

Plaça Nova

C de la Palla

C dels Boters

BARRI GÒTIC

C del Pi

C de la Portaferrissa

C del Duc de la Victoria

C d'en Bot

Caelum

Satan's Coffee Corner

19 🏛

C del Petritxol

Granja

La Pallaresa

C d'en Roca

La Rambla de Sant Josep

La Rambla de Canaletes

La Rambla dels Estudis

C del Pintor Fortuny

C del Carme

15 ✗

Mercat de la Boqueria 🅞

Plaça del Pi

Plaça de Sant Josep Oriol

C del Cardenal Casañas

LA RIBERA

Plaça d'Antoni Maura

Pere rans Baix

C de Sant

Av de Francesc Cambó

Plaça de Ramon Berenguer el Gran

C dels Mercaders

C de les Freixures

C d'en Giralt el Pellisser

C dels Carders

C dels Assaonadors

C de Montcada

C de la Princesa

C de la Bòria

Museu d'Història de Barcelona

Museu Frederic Marès

2 🏛

C dels Comtes

Plaça del Rei

1 🅞

Cereria Subirà

La Llibretería

Plaça de la Seu

Av de la Catedral

La Catedral

Plaça de Sant Felip Neri

Placeta de Manuel Ribé

6 ✗ **10** ✗

El Call

Sinagoga Major

C dels Banys Nous

Sombrereria

Obach

Palau de la Generalitat

C de Sant Honorat

Salterio

Ajuntament

Plaça de Sant Jaume

3 🏛

Basílica dels Sants Màrtirs Just i Pastor

Plaça de Sant Just

Plaça de Jaume I

13 🏛 **4** 🏛

5 ✗

C del Sots-Tinent Navarro

Via Laietana

C de l'Argenteria

C de Manresa

C Vigatans

C de la Nau

C d'A J Baixiras

Casa Gispert

Plaça de Sants Màrtirs

C dels Lledó

C del Correu Vell

C de la Dagueria

14

C de la Ciutat

Plaça de Sant Miquel

C del Pas de l'Ensenyança

C del Call

Baixada de Santa Eulàlia

17 ♿

Plaça dels Traginers

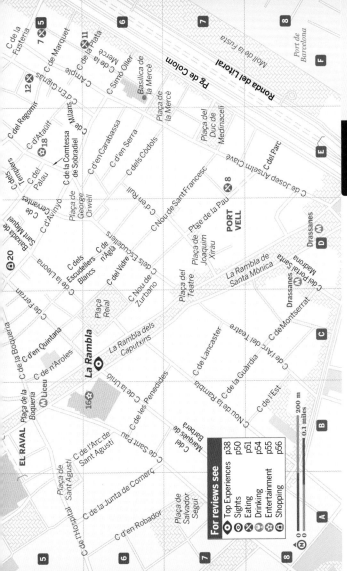

La Rambla & Barri Gòtic

For reviews see

◆	Top Experiences	p38
⊙	Sights	p50
✕	Eating	p51
⊙	Drinking	p54
⊙	Entertainment	p55
⊙	Shopping	p56

200 m
0.1 miles

EL RAVAL

PORT VELL

Port de Barcelona

Sights

Museu d'Història de Barcelona
MUSEUM

1 MAP P48, E3

One of Barcelona's most fascinating museums travels back through the centuries to the very foundations of Roman Barcino. You'll stroll over ruins of the old streets, sewers, laundries, baths and wine- and fish-making factories that flourished here following the town's founding by Emperor Augustus around 10 BCE. Equally impressive is the building itself, which was once part of the Palau Reial Major (Grand Royal Palace) on Plaça del Rei (p47), among the key locations of medieval princely power in Barcelona. (MUHBA;

📞93 256 21 00; http://ajuntament. barcelona.cat/museuhistoria; Plaça del Rei; adult/concession/child €7/5/free, 3-8pm Sun & 1st Sun of month free; ⏱10am-7pm Tue-Sat, to 8pm Sun; Ⓜ Jaume I)

Museu Frederic Marès
MUSEUM

2 MAP P48, D2

The wealthy Catalan sculptor, traveller and obsessive collector Frederic Marès i Deulovol (1893–1991) amassed one of the wildest collections of historical curios. Today, his astonishing displays of religious art and antiques (which he donated to the city of Barcelona) await inside this vast medieval complex, once part of the royal palace of the counts of Barcelona. A rather worn coat of arms on the wall indicates

El Call

One of the most atmospheric parts of the Ciutat Vella is El Call (pronounced 'kye'), the medieval Jewish quarter that flourished here until a tragic 14th-century pogrom. Today its narrow lanes conceal what some historians consider to be the city's main medieval **synagogue** (Map p48, D4; 📞93 317 07 90; www.sinagogamayor.com; Carrer de Marlet 5; adult/child €3.50/free; ⏱10.30am-2.30pm & 3.45-6.30pm Mon-Fri, to 3pm Sun approx Nov-Mar, 10.30am-6.30pm Mon-Fri, to 3pm Sun approx Apr-Oct; Ⓜ Liceu) and the remains of an old Jewish weaver's **house** (Map p48, C4; 📞93 256 21 22; http://ajuntament.barcelona.cat/museuhistoria; Placeta de Manuel Ribé; adult/concession/child €2/1.50/free, 3-7pm Sun & 1st Sun of month free; ⏱11am-2pm Wed, to 7pm Sat & Sun; Ⓜ Jaume I). The boundaries of the **Call Major** are roughly Carrer del Call, Carrer dels Banys Nous, Baixada de Santa Eulàlia and Carrer de Sant Honorat; another pocket, the **Call Menor**, extended across the modern Carrer de Ferran as far as Baixada de Sant Miquel and Carrer d'en Rauric.

that it was also, for a while, the seat of the Spanish Inquisition in Barcelona. (☎93 256 35 00; www.museumares.bcn.cat; Plaça de Sant Iu 5; adult/concession/child €4.20/2.40/free, 3-8pm Sun & 1st Sun of month free; ⏱10am-7pm Tue-Sat, 11am-8pm Sun; Ⓜ Jaume I)

Plaça de Sant Jaume SQUARE

3 ◉ MAP P48, D4

In the 2000 or so years since the Romans settled here, the area around this often-remodelled square, which started life as the forum, has been the focus of Barcelona's civic life – and it's still the central staging area for Barcelona's traditional festivals. Facing each other across the square are the Palau de la Generalitat (http://presidencia.gencat.cat), seat of Catalonia's regional government, on the north side and Barcelona's **Ajuntament** (Casa de la Ciutat; Map p48, D4; ☎93 402 70 00; www.bcn.cat; Plaça de Sant Jaume; admission free; ⏱10am-2pm Sun; Ⓜ Jaume I) on the south. (Ⓜ Liceu, Jaume I)

Basílica dels Sants Màrtirs Just i Pastor CHURCH

4 ◉ MAP P48, E4

This slightly neglected single-nave church, with chapels on either side of the buttressing, was built in 1342 in Catalan Gothic style on what is reputedly the site of the oldest parish church in Barcelona. Inside, you can admire some fine stained-glass windows, then climb the bell tower (closed Sunday)

for knockout views across central Barcelona. In front of it, in a pretty little square that was used as a film set (a smelly Parisian marketplace) in 2006 for *Perfume: The Story of a Murderer,* is what's claimed to be the city's oldest Gothic fountain. (☎93 301 74 33; www.basilicasantjust.cat; Plaça de Sant Just; ⏱11am-2pm & 5-9pm Mon-Sat, 10am-1pm Sun; Ⓜ Jaume I)

Eating

Cafè de l'Acadèmia CATALAN €€

5 🍴 MAP P48, E4

Smartly executed traditional Catalan dishes with the odd creative twist and excellent regional wines make this wood-beamed, stone-walled spot a packed-out local favourite, with tables also on Plaça de Sant Just. City-hall workers pounce on the lunchtime *menú del día* (€16 – or €12 at the bar!), which might mean pear-and-parmesan salad, vegetable rice with Mahón cheese or grilled sole. (☎93 319 82 53; cafedelaacademia@hotmail.com; Carrer dels Lledó 1; mains €10-20; ⏱1-4pm & 8-11pm Mon-Fri, closed Aug; 🛜; Ⓜ Jaume I)

La Vinateria del Call SPANISH €€

6 🍴 MAP P48, D4

In a magical, rambling setting in the former Jewish quarter, this tiny candlelit jewel-box of a wine bar serves up divine Iberian sharing plates dancing from Galician-style octopus and cider-cooked chorizo to perfect *truites* (omelettes)

Els Quatre Gats

Once the lair of Barcelona's Modernista artists, **Els Quatre Gats** (Map p48, B1; ☎93 302 41 40; www.4gats.com; Carrer de Montsió 3; mains €18-38; ☉restaurant 1-4pm & 7pm-midnight, cafe 9am-1am; MUrquinaona) is a stunning example of the movement, inside and out, with its colourful patterned tiles, geometric brickwork and wooden fittings designed by Josep Puig i Cadafalch. The local-focused cuisine (grilled meats, rice dishes, seafood tapas) isn't as thrilling as the setting, but you can just have coffee and a croissant.

and Catalan *escalivada* (roasted peppers, aubergine and onions). Spot-on service, super-fresh local ingredients and a wonderful selection of wines and artisan cheeses from across Spain. (☎93 302 60 92; www.lavinateriadelcall.com; Carrer Salomó Ben Adret 9; raciones €7-18; ☉7.30pm-1am; ☎; MJaume I)

Belmonte   TAPAS €€

7 🍴 MAP P48, F5

Run by two welcoming sisters, this tiny, down-to-earth rust-walled bodega in the southern Barri Gòtic whips up beautifully prepared Tarragona-style small plates rooted in homegrown ingredients from the family garden. Try the excellent *truita*, beautifully rich

patatons (salted new potatoes) with *romesco* or sliced chillies and courgette carpaccio topped with olive oil and goat's cheese, plus the house-made vermouth (€2.75). (☎93 310 76 84; Carrer de la Mercè 29; tapas €5-12; ☉7pm-midnight Tue-Thu, 1-3.30pm & 7pm-midnight Fri & Sat; ☎; MJaume I)

Federal   CAFE €

8 🍴 MAP P48, E7

Brick-walled industrial-chic design, a sea of open MacBooks, stacks of design mags – this welcoming, queue-out-the-door branch of the Sant Antoni Federal (p155) mothership delivers outrageously popular Australian-inspired brunches in a calming glassed-in space overlooking a quiet square. It's known for creative dishes such as baked eggs with spinach and gruyère, avocado toast with carrot hummus and French toast with berry compote. (☎93 280 81 71; www.federalcafe.es; Passatge de la Pau 11; mains €7-10; ☉9am-11pm Mon-Sat, to 5pm Sun; ☎; MDrassanes)

Koy Shunka   JAPANESE €€€

9 🍴 MAP P48, C1

Down a narrow lane north of La Catedral, chef Hideki Matsuhisa's Michelin-starred Koy Shunka opens a portal to sensational dishes from the East – mouth-watering sushi, sashimi, seared Wagyu beef and richly flavoured seaweed salads are served alongside inventive fusion specialities. Don't miss the tender signature tuna belly. (☎93

412 79 39; www.koyshunka.com; Carrer de Copons 7; tasting menus €93-137; 1.30-2.30pm & 8.30-10.30pm Tue-Sat; Urquinaona)

Levante
MEDITERRANEAN €€

10 MAP P48, C4

A snug, stylish and sunny space tucked into the old Call, Levante specialises in beautifully prepped sharing plates that delicately fuse Mediterranean and Middle Eastern flavours: spicy roast-carrot salad, coriander-infused shakshuka, zesty hummus with pomegranate, kumquats and pillowy pita. Polished-concrete floors and dangling plants grace the interior, and vegan and vegetarian options abound, as do natural wines and brunchy bites. (93 858 26 79; www.bistrotlevante.com; Placeta de Manuel Ribé 1; mains €10-13; 10am-midnight; ; Jaume I)

La Plata
TAPAS €

11 MAP P48, F6

Tucked away in a narrow lane near the waterfront, tile-walled La Plata is a humble, well-loved bodega that has served just four simple, perfect plates since launching back in 1945: *pescadito frito* (fried fish), *butifarra* (sausage), anchovies and tomato salad. Throw in the drinkable, affordable wines and vermouth, and you have the makings of a fine, popular tapas spot. (93 315 10 09; www.barlaplata.com; Carrer de la Mercè 28; tapas €2.50-5; 10am-3.15pm & 6.15-11pm Mon-Sat; Jaume I)

Els Quatre Gats

Barri Gòtic
Cafes

Caelum (Map p48, C3; ☑ 93 302 69 93; www.facebook.com/Caelum Barcelona; Carrer de la Palla 8; ⏱10am-8.30pm Mon-Thu, to 9pm Fri-Sun; 🛜; Ⓜ Liceu) An exquisite medieval space serving sweets made by Spanish nuns.

Salterio (Map p48, D4; ☑ 93 302 50 28; www.facebook.com/teteriasal terio; Carrer de Salomó Ben Adret 4; ⏱noon-midnight; 🛜; Ⓜ Jaume I) Moroccan mint teas, Turkish coffees, Mediterranean bites.

Satan's Coffee Corner (Map p48, C4; ☑ 666 222 599; www.satans coffee.com; Carrer de l'Arc de Sant Ramón del Call 11; ⏱9am-6pm Mon-Fri, from 10am Sat & Sun; Ⓜ Liceu, Jaume I) Punk-inspired Satan's is firmly about the locally roasted coffee.

Granja La Pallaresa (Map p48, B4; ☑ 93 302 20 36; Carrer del Petritxol 11; ⏱9am-1pm & 4-9pm Mon-Sat, 9am-1pm & 5-9pm Sun, closed Jul; 🛜; Ⓜ Liceu) Dating to the 1940s, La Pallaresa specialises in crispy *xurros*.

Milk

INTERNATIONAL €

12 MAP P48, F5

Also loved for its crafted cocktails, Irish-run Milk rescues Barcelona night owls with morning-after brunches (until 4.30pm!). Arrive early or join the wait list for lemon-dusted avocado toast, banana pancakes, egg-white omelettes stuffed with *piquillo* peppers and other deliciously rich hangover-beating dishes. It's all served in a cosy lounge with ornate wallpaper, framed prints and cushioned seating. (☑ 93 268 09 22; www.milkbarcelona.com; Carrer d'en Gignàs 21; mains €9-13; ⏱9am-2am Thu-Mon, to 2.30am Fri & Sat; 🛜; Ⓜ Jaume I)

Drinking

Bar Zim

WINE BAR

13 ☕ MAP P48, E4

At this teensy, intimate, cavern-like bar, Catalan (Penedès, Empordà) and lesser-known Spanish wines (glass €3.60) take centre stage, below beamed ceilings. Pair your wine with one of the delicate platters of local cheeses or cold cuts with artisan jams — now *this* is why you really came to Barcelona in the first place. (www.formatgerialaseu.com; Carrer de la Dagueria 20; ⏱6-11pm Mon-Sat; Ⓜ Jaume I)

L'Ascensor
COCKTAIL BAR

14 🔘 MAP P48, E4

Named after the lift (elevator) doors that serve as the front entrance, this clandestine drinking hideout – with its brick ceilings, vintage mirrors and marble-topped tables – gathers a faithful crowd for old-fashioned cocktails (from €7) and lively conversation against a soundtrack of up-tempo jazz and funk. (📞 93 318 53 47; Carrer de la Bellafila 3; ⏱ 6pm-2.30am Sun-Thu, to 3am Fri & Sat; 🛜; Ⓜ Jaume I)

Bar Boadas
COCKTAIL BAR

15 🔘 MAP P48, A2

One of Barcelona's oldest cocktail bars, Boadas is famed for its daiquiris. Amid old monochrome photos and a polished-wood bar, bow-tied waiters have been mixing unique, deliciously drinkable creations since Miguel Boadas opened it in 1933 – Miró and Hemingway both drank here. Miguel was born in Havana, where he was the first barman at the immortal El Floridita. (📞 93 318 95 92; www.boadascocktails.com; Carrer dels Tallers 1; ⏱ noon-2am Mon-Thu, to 3am Fri & Sat; Ⓜ Catalunya)

Entertainment

Gran Teatre del Liceu
THEATRE

16 ⭐ MAP P48, B6

Barcelona's grand old opera house, skilfully restored after a fire in 1994, is one of the world's most technologically advanced theatres. Taking a seat in its grand auditorium, returned to all its 19th-century

Gran Teatre del Liceu

glory but with the very latest in acoustics, you'll time-travel to another age, or alternatively, join a guided **tour** (☎93 485 99 00; 45min tour adult/child €9/free) to explore its architectural beauty. (☎902 787397; www.liceubarcelona. cat; La Rambla 51-59; tickets €15-250; Ⓜ Liceu)

El Paraigua   LIVE MUSIC

17 ⭐ MAP P48, D4

A tiny chocolate box of dark tinted Modernisme, the 'Umbrella' has been serving up drinks since the 1960s. But downstairs in the moody basement, travel from Modernisme to medieval amid 11th-century brick walls. Live bands – funk, soul, rock, blues, flamenco – regularly hold court on Friday and Saturday (check

Traditional bakery on Ramblas St

DAVID PEREIRAS/SHUTTERSTOCK ©

schedules online). (☎93 317 14 79; www.elparaigua.com; Carrer del Pas de l'Enssenyança 2; admission free; ⏱noon-midnight Sun-Thu, to 3am Fri & Sat; Ⓜ Liceu)

Harlem Jazz Club   JAZZ

18 ⭐ MAP P48, E5

This narrow, old-city dive is one of the best spots in town for jazz, as well as funk, Latin, blues and gypsy jazz, and attracts a mixed crowd that maintains a respect-ful silence during performances. Most concerts start at 10.30pm or 11pm; get in early if you want a seat in front of the stage. (☎93 310 07 55; www.harlemjazzclub.es; Carrer de la Comtessa de Sobradiel 8; tickets €8-12; ⏱8pm-3am Sun & Tue-Thu, to 5am Fri & Sat; Ⓜ Jaume I)

Shopping

L'Arca   CLOTHING

19 🔒 MAP P48, C4

Step inside this enchanting vintage boutique for beautifully crafted apparel from the past, mostly sourced from local homes: 18th-century embroidered silk vests, elaborate silk kimonos and 1920s shawls and wedding dresses, plus old-style earrings made by artisans in southern Spain. The incredible collection has provided fashion for films including *Titanic, Talk to Her* and *Perfume: The Story of a Mur-derer.* (☎93 302 15 98; www.larca.es; Carrer dels Banys Nous 20; ⏱11am-2pm & 4-8pm Mon-Sat; Ⓜ Liceu)

Preserving Barcelona's Historic Shops

From centuries-old candle-makers to family bakeries, Barcelona's traditional, historical, specialist shops are just as key to the city's soul as Gaudí's Modernista creations. Over the last few years, however, some of the best-known shops have been forced to close, largely down to rising rents (in some cases linked to growing numbers of tourist apartments pushing up prices). But it's certainly not all lost: in 2015, 228 stores across Barcelona were given a special preservation status, which means that their original facades and interiors can't be altered; 32 of these can't be changed at all. Visitors can show their support by shopping at much-loved Barcelona icons such as bakeries **Escribà** (p41) and **La Colmena** (Map p48, E3; 93 315 13 56; www.pastisserialacolmena.com; Plaça de l'Angel 12; 9am-9pm; Jaume I), hat-maker **Sombrerería Obach** (Map p48, C4; 93 318 40 94; www.sombreriaobach.es; Carrer del Call 2; 10am-2pm & 4-8pm Mon-Fri, 10am-2pm & 4.30-8pm Sat Oct-Jul, 10am-2pm & 4-8pm Mon-Fri, 10am-2pm Sat Aug-Sep; Jaume I), candle-producer **Cerería Subirà** (Map p48, E3; 93 315 26 06; www.cereriasubira.cat; Baixada de la Llibreteria 7; 10am-2pm & 4-8pm Mon-Sat Jun-Sep, 9.30am-1.30pm & 4-8pm Mon & Tue, 9.30am-8pm Wed-Sat Oct-May; Jaume I), or dried-fruit specialist **Casa Gispert** (p91).

La Manual Alpargatera   SHOES

20 🔒 MAP P48, D5

Stars from Salvador Dalí to Penélope Cruz and Jean Paul Gaultier have ordered a pair of *espardenyes* (espadrilles; rope-soled canvas shoes) from this famous shoe specialist, founded just after the Spanish Civil War. The roots of the simple design date back hundreds of years and originated in the Catalan Pyrenees, though La Manual also incorporates contemporary trends. (93 301 01 72; www.lamanualalpargatera.es; Carrer d'Avinyó 7; 9.30am-8pm Mon-Fri, from 10am Sat; Liceu)

Explore ◈

El Raval

The once down-and-out district of El Raval is still seedy in parts, though it has seen remarkable rejuvenation in recent years, with the addition of cutting-edge museums and cultural centres, such as Richard Meier's MACBA. This is one of Barcelona's most vibrant and multicultural districts, and what El Raval lacks in block-buster sights it makes up for with plenty of louche charm, historical bars and trendy cafes, restaurants and boutiques.

The Short List

○ **MACBA (p63)** *Getting to grips with the occasion-ally challenging art collection and watching skaters perform their tricks out the front.*

○ **Antic Hospital de la Santa Creu (p64)** *Exploring this historic building, where Gaudí died, and relaxing under the trees in its elegant courtyard.*

○ **Bars (p68)** *Admiring some lesser-known works of Modernisme such as Casa Almirall, or seeking out avant-garde cocktails at stylish new arrivals like Two Schmucks.*

○ **Palau Güell (p63)** *Walking around this artfully restored Gaudí-designed palace.*

○ **Dinner time! (p65)** *Diving into Barcelona's most multicultural food scene, from superb tacos at El Pachuco to classic Catalan at Elisabets.*

Getting There

Ⓜ Línies 1, 2 and 3 stop at strategic points around El Raval, so nothing is far from a metro stop. The Línia 3 stop at Liceu and the Línia 2 stop at Sant Antoni are handy.

Neighbourhood Map on p62

Palau Güell (p63) ALIONABIRUKOVA/SHUTTERSTOCK ©

Walking Tour 🚶

Revelling in El Raval

El Raval is a neighbourhood whose contradictory impulses are legion. This journey through the local life of the barri takes you from haunts beloved by the savvy young professionals moving into the area to gritty streetscapes and one-time slums. En route, we stop at places that, unlike much of the neighbourhood, haven't changed in decades.

Walk Facts

Start Kasparo;
Ⓜ Catalunya

End Bar Marsella;
Ⓜ Liceu

Length 2.5km; all day

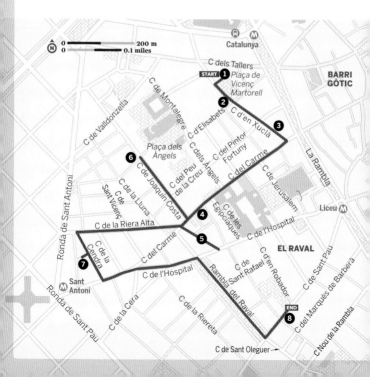

❶ Kasparo

Friendly terrace cafe **Kasparo** (📞93 302 20 72; www.kasparo.es; Plaça de Vicenç Martorell 4; mains €7-12; ⏰9am-11pm or midnight Tue-Sat; 📶; Ⓜ️Catalunya), overlooking traffic-free Plaça de Vicenç Martorell from beneath the arches, is a favourite with local parents.

❷ Elisabets

Northern El Raval is rapidly gentrifying, but places like brilliant **Elisabets** (📞93 317 58 26; Carrer de les Ramelleres 1; tapas €3-10, mains €8-10; ⏰7.30am-11.30pm Mon-Thu & Sat, to 1.30am Fri Sep-Jul, closed mid-Jul–mid-Aug; Ⓜ️Catalunya), loved for its good-value cooking, hold firm. The *menú del dia* (€12) changes daily, or try the tapas.

❸ Granja M Viader

For over a century, people have been coming to classically Catalan milk bar **Granja M Viader** (📞93 318 34 86; www.granjaviader.cat; Carrer d'en Xuclà 6; ⏰9am-1.15pm & 5-9pm Mon-Sat; Ⓜ️Liceu) for hot chocolate ladled out with whipped cream (ask for a *suís*).

❹ Bar Muy Buenas

Now serving impressive cocktails and Catalan dishes, Modernista classic **Bar Muy Buenas** (📞93 807 28 57; www.muybuenas.cat; Carrer del Carme 63; mains €9-15; ⏰1-3.30pm & 8-11pm Mon-Thu, 1-4pm & 8pm-midnight Fri, 1pm-midnight Sat, 1-11.30pm Sun; Ⓜ️Liceu) has been a bar since 1928, and wears its past proudly

with stunning original woodwork, etched windows and a marble bar.

❺ Carrer de la Riera Baixa

Little more than 100m long, **Carrer de la Riera Baixa** is known for its vintage fashion shops.

❻ Casa Almirall

In business since 1860, corner bar **Casa Almirall** (📞93 318 99 17; www.casaalmirall.com; Carrer de Joaquín Costa 33; ⏰4.30pm-1.30am Mon, 4pm-2.30am Tue & Wed, noon-2.30am Thu, noon-3am Fri & Sat, noon-12.30am Sun; 📶; Ⓜ️Universitat) is dark and intriguing, with Modernista decor, a mixed clientele, and absinthe and vermouth on the menu.

❼ JazzSí Club

A cramped little bar run by the Taller de Músics (Musicians' Workshop) school and foundation, **JazzSí Club** (📞93 329 00 20; www.tallerdemusics.com; Carrer de Requesens 2; entry incl drink €6-12; ⏰8.30-11pm Mon & Thu, 7.45-11pm Tue & Wed, 8.45-11pm Fri & Sat, 6.30-10pm Sun; Ⓜ️Sant Antoni) has offerings from jazz jams to good flamenco (Friday and Saturday).

❽ Bar Marsella

Wander down the Rambla del Raval to reach **Bar Marsella** (📞93 442 72 63; Carrer de Sant Pau 65; ⏰6pm-2am Mon-Thu, 10pm-3am Fri, 6pm-2.30am Sat, 10pm-2.30am Sun; Ⓜ️Liceu). Going since 1820, this *absenta* (absinthe) specialist has served the likes of Dalí, Picasso, Gaudí and Hemingway.

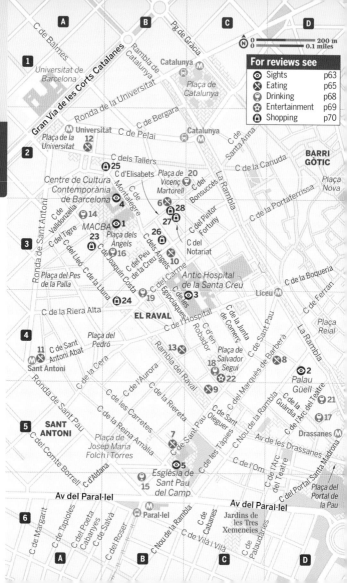

El Raval

C de Balmes
Universitat de Barcelona
Gran Via de les Corts Catalanes
Rambla de Catalunya
Pg de Gràcia
Catalunya Ⓜ
Plaça de Catalunya
Ronda de la Universitat
C de Bergara
C de Pelai
Universitat Ⓜ 12
Plaça de la Universitat
Catalunya Ⓜ
C de Santa Anna
BARRI GÒTIC
C dels Tallers
C d'Elisabets
Plaça de Vicenç Martorell 20
C de la Canuda
Plaça Nova
Centre de Cultura Contemporània de Barcelona 4
C de Montalegre
6 28
C del Bonsuccés
C del Pintor Fortuny
C de la Portaferrissa
14
MACBA 1
Plaça dels Àngels
23
16
26
27
C del Notariat
C del Pes de la Palla
24
19
Antic Hospital de la Santa Creu 3
C de la Boqueria
Liceu Ⓜ
C de Ferran
Plaça Reial
11 C de Sant Antoni Abat
Sant Antoni Ⓜ
Plaça del Pedró
13
Plaça de Salvador Seguí
18 22
9
8
2 Palau Güell
21
17
Drassanes Ⓜ
SANT ANTONI
Plaça de Josep Maria Folch i Torres
7
5
15
Església de Sant Pau del Camp
Av del Paral·lel
Paral·lel Ⓜ
Jardins de les Tres Xemeneies
Plaça del Portal de la Pau

For reviews see
- Sights p63
- Eating p65
- Drinking p68
- Entertainment p69
- Shopping p70

Sights

MACBA

GALLERY

1  MAP P62, B3

An extraordinary all-white, glass-fronted creation by American architect Richard Meier, opened in 1995, the MACBA has become the city's foremost contemporary art centre, with captivating exhibitions for the serious art lover. The permanent collection is dedicated to Spanish and Catalan art from the second half of the 20th century, with works by Antoni Tàpies, Joan Brossa, Miquel Barceló and Joan Rabascall. International artists, such as Paul Klee, Bruce Nauman, Alexander Calder, John Cage and Jean-Michel Basquiat, are also represented. (Museu d'Art Contemporani de Barcelona; 93 412 08 10; www.macba.cat; Plaça dels Àngels 1; adult/concession/child under 14yr €11/8.80/free, 4-8pm Sat free; 11am-7.30pm Mon & Wed-Fri, 10am-8pm Sat, 10am-3pm Sun & public holidays; Universitat)

Palau Güell

PALACE

2 MAP P62, D4

Built off La Rambla in the late 1880s for Gaudí's wealthy patron the industrialist Eusebi Güell, the Palau Güell is a magnificent example of the early days of the architect's fevered architectural imagination. This extraordinary neo-Gothic mansion (one of few major buildings of that era raised in Ciutat Vella) gives an insight into its maker's prodigious genius, and, though a little sombre compared

Fernando Botero's 'El Gat de Botero', Rambla del Raval (p65)

Festes de la Mercè

The city's biggest party involves four days of concerts, dancing and street theatre held at various locations across town around 24 September. There are also *castells* (human towers), a fireworks display synchronised with the Montjuïc fountains, a parade of *gegants* (papier-mâché giants), and *correfocs* (fireworks-spitting monsters and demons).

with some of his later whims, it's a characteristic riot of styles (Gothic, Islamic, art nouveau) and materials. (📞93 472 57 75; www.palauguell.cat; Carrer Nou de la Rambla 3-5; adult/concession/child under 10yr incl audio guide €12/9/free, 1st Sun of month free; 🕑10am-8pm Tue-Sun Apr-Oct, to 5.30pm Nov-Mar; Ⓜ Drassanes)

Antic Hospital de la Santa Creu   HISTORIC BUILDING

3 ⓞ MAP P62, C4

Behind the Mercat de La Boqueria stands the Gothic Antic Hospital de la Santa Creu, which was once the city's main hospital. Founded in 1401, it functioned until the 1930s, and was considered one of the best in Europe in its medieval heyday – it is famously the place where Antoni Gaudí died in 1926. Today it houses the **Biblioteca de Catalunya**, with its distinctive Gothic arches, and the **Institut**

d'Estudis Catalans (📞93 270 16 20; www.iec.cat; Carrer del Carme 47; 🕑tours 10.30am, 11.30am & 12.30pm Tue & Thu; Ⓜ Liceu). (Former Hospital of the Holy Cross; Carrer de l'Hospital 56; admission free; 🕑9am-10pm; Ⓜ Liceu)

Centre de Cultura Contemporània de Barcelona   GALLERY

4 ⓞ MAP P62, B2

A complex of auditoriums, exhibition spaces and conference halls, the CCCB opened in 1994 in what was formerly an 18th-century hospice, the Casa de la Caritat. Its courtyard, with a vast glass wall on one side, is spectacular. With 4500 sq metres of galleries in four separate areas, the centre hosts a constantly changing programme of exhibitions, film cycles and other events. (CCCB; 📞93 306 41 00; www.cccb.org; Carrer de Montalegre 5; adult/concession/child under 12yr €6/4/free, 3-8pm Sun free; 🕑11am-8pm Tue-Sun; Ⓜ Universitat)

Església de Sant Pau del Camp   CHURCH

5 ⓞ MAP P62, B5

The best example of Romanesque architecture in Barcelona is the dainty little cloister of this small 11th- or 12th-century church, which was founded in the 9th or 10th century but later rebuilt. The cloister's 13th-century poly-lobulated arches, sitting atop intricately carved capitals, are unique in Europe. The church itself contains the tombstone of Guifré II, son of Guifré el Pelós, a 9th-century count considered the founding father of Catalonia. (☎93 441 00 01; www.santpaudelcamp. org; Carrer de Sant Pau 101; adult/ concession/child under 14yr €5/4/free; ⏱10am-2pm & 3-6pm Mon-Sat, 10am-1pm Sun; Ⓜ Paral·lel)

Eating

Bar Central
CAFE €

6 🍴 MAP P62, B3

Launched in 2019 by the superstar foodie teams behind Barcelona hits Satan's Coffee (p54) and Xemei (p163), this fabulous tucked-away cafe-bar has taken over the palm-studded, ivy-wreathed courtyard and gardens and the priest's house of the 16th-century Casa de la Misericòrdia (a former orphanage). Classic coffees and vermouths accompany perfectly flaky croissants and delicate *entrepans* and salads. (Carrer d'Elisabets 6; snacks €2-7; ⏱10am-9pm; Ⓜ Catalunya)

El Pachuco
MEXICAN €

7 🍴 MAP P62, B5

Get to El Pachuco early or jump on the wait list – this tiny, narrow and deservedly popular *mezcalería/taquería* gets completely packed with a low-key fashionable crowd. Exposed lightbulbs, dim lighting, bar stools and shelves cluttered with booze bottles and religious icons set the scene for first-rate

tacos, quesadillas, guacamole and margaritas. There's a more spacious sister branch, **La Pachuca** (www.facebook.com/LaPachucaBcn; Carrer d'en Carabassa 19; mains €7-9; ⏱1.30pm-2am Tue-Sun; Ⓜ Jaume I, Barceloneta) in Barri Gòtic. (www.facebook.com/pachucobcn; Carrer de Sant Pau 110; dishes €6-11; ⏱1.30pm-2am Mon-Thu, to 2.30am Fri-Sun; Ⓜ Paral·lel)

Cañete
TAPAS €€

8 🍴 MAP P62, D4

Epitomising the ongoing trend in smartened-up versions of traditional tapas bars, much-loved and always-busy Cañete centres on a bustling open kitchen with a marble-topped bar. The long list

---

Rambla del Raval

This **broad boulevard** (Ⓜ Liceu) was laid out in 2000 as part of the city's plan to open up this formerly sleazy neighbourhood. The plan certainly proved to have some success. Now lined with palm trees and terrace cafes, the Rambla del Raval hosts a craft market every weekend and is presided over by the glossy Barceló Raval hotel. Fernando Botero's 7m-long, 2m-tall bronze sculpture of a plump cat, *El Gat de Botero*, is something of a Barcelona icon.

El Raval Dining

El Raval's great-value dining scene roams across the globe. Timeless Barcelona classics are scattered across what was long the old city's poorest *barri* (district), while battalions of arty bars and restaurants dot the area around the MACBA and Carrer de Joaquín Costa. There are some great vegan and vegetarian dining spots, too.

of uberfresh tapas and *platillos* (sharing plates) packs in an impressive bunch of modern twists (such as wild-tuna tataki with seaweed) alongside traditional favourites, including gooey tortilla and Andalucian classics such as *boquerones* (anchovies) and *tortillitas de camarones* (shrimp fritters). (📞93 270 34 58; www.barcanete.com; Carrer de la Unió 17; tapas €2-15, sharing plates €7-22; 🕐1pm-midnight Mon-Sat; 🛜; Ⓜ Liceu)

Suculent   CATALAN €€

9 🍴 MAP P62, C5

Part of celebrity chef Carles Abellán's culinary empire, this old-style bistro showcases the best of contemporary Catalan cuisine courtesy of El Bulli–trained chef Toni Romero. From tantalising mixes such as red-prawn ceviche with avocado to steak tartare over grilled bone marrow, only the very finest ingredients make it into the smartly executed creations. (📞93 443 65 79; www.suculent.com; Rambla del Raval 45; mains €11-18, tasting menus €45-97; 🕐1-4pm & 8-11.30pm Wed-Sun; 🛜; Ⓜ Liceu)

Caravelle   INTERNATIONAL €

10 🍴 MAP P62, B3

Beloved of El Raval's stylish crowd and anyone with a discerning palate, this soulful little cafe-restaurant dishes up seasonally changing tacos like you've never tasted (cod, lime aioli and radish, roast pumpkin with frijoles) and creative international-style brunches that see queues snaking out the door. Coffee comes from Nømad (p68), while craft beers are home-brewed. (📞93 317 98 92; www.caravelle.es; Carrer del Pintor Fortuny 31; mains €7-15; 🕐9am-5pm Mon, to midnight Tue-Fri, 10am-midnight Sat, 10am-5pm Sun approx May-Sep, reduced hours Oct-Apr; 🛜; Ⓜ Liceu)

Sésamo   VEGETARIAN €

11 🍴 MAP P62, A4

Regularly lauded as one of the best veggie restaurants in the city, fun and cosy Sésamo transforms fresh, local ingredients into artful tapas: goat's-cheese salad, puff-pastry filled with feta and spinach, mushroom croquettes and more. Most people go for the seven-course tapas menu (vegetarian/vegan €25/30, wine included, minimum two people). Nice touches include the home-baked bread and cakes. (📞93 441 64 11;

Carrer de Sant Antoni Abat 52; tapas €4-7, mains €9-14; ⏱7pm-midnight; 🛜📶; Ⓜ Sant Antoni)

Flax & Kale HEALTH FOOD €€

12 MAP P62, A2

Catalan chef Teresa Carles' self-styled 'healthy flexitarian restaurant' is a chic, sprawling, palm-dotted world where 80% of the menu is plant-based (20% comprises oily fish) and the all-round emphasis is on nutrition. Raw, vegan and gluten-free options abound; dishes wander from açai bowls and red-quinoa pancakes to grilled-aubergine ravioli and Panang red curry. Head upstairs for the leafy terrace. (📞93 317 56 64; www.teresacarles.com; Carrer dels Tallers 74b; mains €11-18;

9am-11.30pm Mon-Fri, from 9.30am Sat & Sun; 🛜📶; Ⓜ Universitat)

Casa Leopoldo CATALAN €€

13 MAP P62, B4

Relaunched in 2017 by chefs Óscar Manresa and Romain Fornell, yet staying true to its classic roots, this charming El Raval old-timer has tile-patterned walls, bullfighting posters and smart white table-cloths. The kitchen showcases traditional Catalan favourites such as *cap i pota* (beef-and-chickpea stew) and oxtail in red wine, along with fried prawns, wild mushrooms and other deliciously uncomplicated tapas. (📞93 441 30 14; www.casaleopoldo.es; Carrer de Sant Rafael 24; tapas €4-15, mains €12-19; ⏱1-4pm & 8pm-late, closed Aug)

MACBA (p63)

El Raval street scene

Drinking

Two Schmucks
COCKTAIL BAR

14   MAP P62, A3

Originally a wandering pop-up bar, seriously edgy yet refreshingly unpretentious Swedish-run Two Schmucks has become one of Barcelona's (and Europe's) most talked-about cocktail bars, with ambitious owner-bartenders Moe and AJ sweeping multiple awards. Channelling a glammed-up dive-bar vibe, with recycled furniture and a fun friendly team, it mixes outstanding liquid concoctions like the signature Curry Colada (€9). (635 396 088; www.facebook.com/schmuckordie; Carrer de Joaquín Costa 52; 5pm-2am Sun-Fri, to 2.30am Sat; Sant Antoni, Universitat)

La Confiteria
BAR

15   MAP P62, B6

This evocative tile-covered cocktail hang-out is a trip back to the 19th century. Until the 1980s it was a confectioner's shop, and though the original cabinets are now bursting with booze, the look has barely changed with its conversion courtesy of one of Barcelona's foremost teams in nightlife wizardry. The scene these days is lively and creative (drinks €8 to €10). (93 140 54 35; www.confiteria.cat; Carrer de Sant Pau 128; 7pm-2am Mon-Thu, 6pm-3am Fri & Sat, 5pm-2am Sun; ; Paral·lel)

Nømad Every Day
COFFEE

16   MAP P62, B3

A seasonal roster of roasted-in-Barcelona beans combine with the latest caffeine tech at El Raval's branch of super-successful Nømad, founded by rockstar barista Jordi Mestre after a stint on London's coffee scene. Join the city's aficionados for a flat white, cold brew or Aeropress (coffees €2.50 to €5), surrounded by patterned floor tiles, minimal rust-red decor and a living wall. (www.nomadcoffee.es; Carrer de Joaquín Costa 26; 8.30am-6.30pm Mon-Fri, 10am-7pm Sat & Sun; Sant Antoni, Universitat)

Bar Pastís
BAR

17   MAP P62, D5

A French-cabaret theme (with lots of Piaf on the stereo) pervades this tiny, cluttered classic, which has been going, on and off, since the end of WWII, when it was founded by a French exile. You'll need to be in before 9pm to have any hope of sitting at or getting near the bar. Frequent live performances usually include French *chanson*. (📞 634 031 527; www.facebook.com/barpastisraval; Carrer de Santa Mònica 4; ⏰ 7.30pm-2am Tue-Sun; 📶; Ⓜ Drassanes)

La Monroe
BAR

18 Ⓜ MAP P62, C4

Peer through the glass walls of this lively LGBTIQ+ friendly hangout inside the Filmoteca de Catalunya, and you'll spot long wooden tables, rickety chairs, leafy plants, industrial touches and a cobbled floor that mimics the square outside. Great cocktails and vermouth, a €12 *menú del dia* and delectable tapas (€4 to €12) such as grilled Huelva prawns and Catalan *fuet* (thin pork sausage). (📞 93 441 94 61; www.lamonroe.es; Plaça Salvador Seguí 1-9; ⏰ noon-late; 📶; Ⓜ Liceu)

33 | 45
BAR

19 Ⓜ MAP P62, B4

A wonderfully low-key yet stylish bar on a street full of them, this busy industrial-chic place has excellent mojitos (€5 to €7), a fashionable crowd and a frequently changing exhibition of art on the walls. There are DJs most nights and cosy sofas for kicking back over coffee. (📞 93 187 41 38; www.facebook.com/3345bar; Carrer de Joaquín Costa 4; ⏰ 5pm-2am Mon, 1pm-2am Tue-Thu, to 2.30am Fri & Sat, to 1.30am Sun; 📶; Ⓜ Sant Antoni)

Caribbean Club
COCKTAIL BAR

20 Ⓜ MAP P62, C2

The dimly lit ship-like interior, with low wooden beams and cocktail shakers and literature displayed in glass cabinets, is just a taster at this elegant cocktail spot headed up by respected barman Juanjo González Rubiera. Caribbean rums steal the show (cocktails €9), while other tempting mixes include a delicate Gin Smash. (📞 93 302 21 82; www.caribbeanclubbcn.com; Carrer de les Sitges 5; ⏰ 6pm-2.30am Tue-Sat; 📶; Ⓜ Catalunya)

Moog
CLUB

21 Ⓜ MAP P62, D5

This fun and minuscule club is a standing favourite with the downtown crowd. In the main dance area, DJs dish out house, techno and electro, while upstairs you can groove to a blend of indie and occasional classic-pop throwbacks. (📞 93 319 17 89; www.moogbarcelona.com; Carrer de l'Arc del Teatre 3; entry €5-10; ⏰ midnight-5am Sun-Thu, to 5.30am Fri & Sat; Ⓜ Drassanes)

Entertainment

Filmoteca de Catalunya
CINEMA

22 ⭐ MAP P62, C4

Relocated to El Raval in 2012 as part of plans to revive the neighbourhood's cultural offerings,

Out & About in El Raval

The shadowy side streets of El Raval are dotted with scores of bars and clubs, and despite its vestigial edginess, this is a great place to go out. You'll find super-fashionable cocktail spots alongside great old taverns that have been the hangouts of the city's bohemia since Picasso's time. Studenty Carrer de Joaquín Costa is a treasure trove of bars old and new. The lower end of El Raval has a history of insalubriousness and the area around Carrer de Sant Pau retains its seedy feel: drug dealers, pickpockets and prostitutes mingle with nocturnal hedonists. Keep your wits about you.

Catalonia's national cinema occupies a modern 6000-sq-metre building in the midst of the most louche part of El Raval. The films shown are a superior mix of classics and more recent releases, with frequent themed cycles. (📞93 567 10 70; www.filmoteca.cat; Plaça de Salvador Seguí 1-9; adult/concession €4/3; ⏰screenings 5-10pm, ticket office 10am-3pm Tue-Fri, plus 4-9.30pm Tue-Thu & Sun, to 10pm Fri & Sat; Ⓜ Liceu)

Shopping

Les Topettes   COSMETICS

23 🔒 MAP P62, A3

Globe-trotting products at this chic little temple to soap and perfume have been handpicked, by journalist Lucía and chef/interior designer Oriol, for their designs as much as for their qualities. You'll find gorgeously packaged scents, candles, soaps and creams from Diptyque, Cowshed and Hierbas de Ibiza, among others. (📞93 500 55 64; www.lestopettes.com; Carrer de Joaquín Costa 33; ⏰4-9pm Mon, 11am-2pm & 4-9pm Tue-Sat; Ⓜ Universitat)

Grey Street   HOMEWARES

24 🔒 MAP P62, B4

Named for the Canberra home of Australian owner Amy Cocker's grandparents, this stylishly reimagined former perfume shop is decked with tempting trinkets, many of them crafted by local or Spanish artists – handpainted ceramic mugs and plant pots, fair-trade incense, tarot cards, patterned wall prints, handmade swimwear, vegan skincare and more. There's another **branch** (Carrer dels Agullers 12; ⏰11am-8.30pm Mon-Sat; Ⓜ Jaume I, Barceloneta) in El Born. (www.greystreet barcelona.com; Carrer Peu de la Creu 25; ⏰11am-3pm & 4-9pm Mon-Sat; Ⓜ Sant Antoni)

Holala! Plaza FASHION & ACCESSORIES

25 🔒 MAP P62, B2

Backing on to Carrer de Vall-donzella, this Ibiza import is inspired by the Balearic island's long-established (and now somewhat commercialised) hippie tradition. Vintage clothes sourced from flea markets and reusable-fashion outlets across the globe are the name of the game, with lots of denim and vibrant colours on show, plus an eclectic exhibitions programme. (📞93 302 05 93; www.holala-ibiza.com; Plaça de Castella 2; ⏰11am-9pm Mon-Sat; Ⓜ Universitat)

Lantoki FASHION & ACCESSORIES

26 🔒 MAP P62, B3

Designers Urko Martinez and Sandra Liberal handcraft their own minimalist women's fashion in this bright, breezy El Raval studio-boutique, which also flaunts pieces by other local creatives. The emphasis is on original, slow-fashion artisan collections, and there are also design-your-own-clothes workshops (around €40 to €90). (www.lantoki.es; Carrer del Doctor Dou 15; ⏰11am-8pm Mon-Fri, from noon Sat; Ⓜ Catalunya, Liceu)

Teranyina ARTS & CRAFTS

27 🔒 MAP P62, B3

Artist Teresa Rosa Aguayo runs this textile workshop in the heart of the artsy bit of El Raval. You can join workshops at the loom,

Specialist Shops

Some of Barcelona's most original shopping is in El Raval. A handful of art galleries surround the MACBA, and there's a healthy secondhand and vintage-clothes scene on Carrer de la Riera Baixa and around. Carrer dels Tallers is one of the city's main music strips, and local fashion designers and interior designers have set up workshops and boutiques all over the *barri*.

admire some of the rugs and other pieces that Teresa has created and, of course, buy them. (📞93 317 94 36; www.textilteranyina.com; Carrer del Notariat 10; ⏰11am-3pm & 5-8pm Mon-Fri; Ⓜ Catalunya)

La Variété HOMEWARES

28 🔒 MAP P62, B3

Decorative pieces made from Chiang Mai wood, lampshades that reuse old bamboo lobster traps and handmade hanging terracotta plant pots are just a few of the tempting home-designed pieces at this calming interiors boutique, which collaborates directly with artists, craftspeople and farmers in Thailand. (📞93 519 83 51; www.lavariete.net; Carrer d'Elisabets 7; ⏰11am-3pm & 4-8.30pm Mon-Sat; Ⓜ Catalunya, Liceu)

Explore ⊚
La Ribera &
El Born

This charming, busy medieval quarter hosts some of the city's liveliest tapas bars and most original boutiques, along with key sights such as the Museu Picasso, the awe-inspiring Basílica de Santa Maria del Mar, the artfully sculpted Palau de la Música Catalana, and the leafy Parc de la Ciutadella.

The Short List

○ **Basílica de Santa Maria del Mar (p78)** *Admiring the simplicity and beauty of this fine example of Catalan Gothic, built with help from local parishioners.*

○ **Museu Picasso (p74)** *Being introduced to the origins of Picasso's genius at this fascinating museum spread across a series of interconnected palaces.*

○ **Palau de la Música Catalana (p84)** *Taking in a show or exploring on a tour of this marvellous Modernista concert hall.*

○ **Bar-hopping in El Born (p81)** *Tucking into old-school tapas and sipping avant-garde cocktails amid El Born's buzz, perhaps at award-winning Dr Stravinsky.*

○ **Parc de la Ciutadella (p84)** *Enjoying a stroll, having a picnic, taking a boat out on the lake and spotting the artworks.*

Getting There

Ⓜ Línia 4 coasts down the southwest flank of La Ribera, stopping at Urquinaona, Jaume I and Barceloneta. Línia 1 also stops nearby, at Urquinaona and Arc de Triomf (the nearest stop for Parc de la Ciutadella).

Neighbourhood Map on p82

House in El Born SKYNEXT/SHUTTERSTOCK ©

Top Experience 📷
Admire the art and surrounds of Museu Picasso

The setting alone, in five contiguous medieval stone mansions, makes Barcelona's Museu Picasso unique (and worth the queues). While the collection concentrates on Pablo Picasso's formative years, there is enough material from subsequent better-known periods to showcase the artist's versatility and genius. You come away feeling that Picasso was the true original, always one step ahead.

📍 MAP P82, D4

📞 93 256 30 00

www.museupicasso.bcn.cat

Carrer de Montcada 15-23

🕙 10am-5pm Mon, 9am-8.30pm Tue, Wed & Fri-Sun, to 9.30pm Thu

History of the Museum

Allegedly it was Picasso himself who proposed the museum's creation in 1960, to his friend and personal secretary Jaume Sabartés, a Barcelona native. Three years later, the 'Sabartés Collection' was opened, since a museum bearing Picasso's name would have been met with censorship – Picasso's opposition to the Franco regime was well known. The Museu Picasso we see today opened in 1983. It originally held only Sabartés' personal collection of Picasso's art and a handful of other works, but the collection gradually expanded with donations from Salvador Dalí and Sebastià Junyer Vidal, among others. However, the largest part of the present collection came from Picasso himself. His widow, Jacqueline Roque, also donated 41 ceramic pieces and the *Woman with Bonnet* painting after Picasso's death.

Sabartés' contribution is honoured with Picasso's famous Blue Period portrait of him wearing a ruff (room B1).

The Collection

The collection, which includes more than 3500 artworks, is strongest on Picasso's earliest years, up until 1904, which is apt considering that the artist spent his formative creative years in Barcelona. What makes this collection truly impressive – one of a kind among the world's many Picasso museums – is the way in which it displays Picasso's extraordinary talent at such a young age. Masterpieces such as the enormous *Ciència i Caritat* or *Retrato de la tía Pepa*, as well as some self-portraits and the portraits of his parents, which date from 1896, shine a light on Picasso's precocious talent.

Early Days

Room 1 holds sketches and oils from Picasso's early years in Málaga and A Coruña (1893–95) and leads on to his formative years

★ **Top Tips**

○ At €15, the Carnet del Museu Picasso annual pass is barely more expensive than a day pass, and allows multiple entries. There is a special desk for this at Carrer de Montcada 23.

○ Avoid queues by booking tickets online and choosing a time slot, or arrive first thing.

○ Tickets for adult/concession/under 18yr, including temporary exhibits, cost €14/7.50/free, while 6-9.30pm Thursday and the 1st Sunday of the month are free

✕ **Take a Break**

Wander north along Carrer de Montcada for traditional-with-a-twist tapas at Bar del Pla (p81).

Euskal Etxea (p81), along the same street, is one of the best *pintxo* bars in town.

★ **Getting There**

Ⓜ Jaume I

in Barcelona. *Retrato de la tía Pepa* (Portrait of Aunt Pepa; room 2), done in Málaga in 1896, shows the maturity of his brush strokes and his ability to portray character – at the tender age of 15. As you walk into room 3, you'll see the enormous *Ciència i caritat* (Science and Charity), painted in 1897; faced with the technical virtuosity of such a painting it seems almost inconceivable that it could have been created by the hands of a 15-year-old.

Catalan Avant-Garde & Blue Period

After a period spent in Horta de Sant Joan, Picasso came to Barcelona and joined what was known as the 'Catalan avant-garde', which you'll see in room 4. In rooms 5 to 7 paintings from 1900–1901 hang, while room 8 is dedicated to the first significant new stage in his development, the Blue Period. *Woman with Bonnet* (1901) is an important work from this period, depicting a detainee from the Saint-Lazare women's prison and venereal disease hospital, which Picasso visited when in Paris – it also sets up the theme of Picasso's fascination with those inhabiting the down-and-out layers of society.

The nocturnal blue-tinted views of *Terrats de Barcelona* (Roofs of Barcelona; room 8) and *El foll* (The Madman; often on loan) are cold and cheerless, yet somehow alive. *Terrats de Barcelona* (1903) is typical of the period, when Picasso frequently painted the city rooftops from different perspectives.

Early Cubism

Picasso did many drawings of beggars, the blind and the impoverished elderly throughout 1903 and 1904.

Museu Picasso

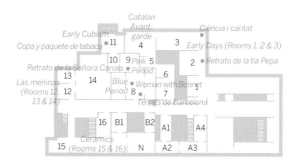

This leads to the 1905 painting of Benedetta Bianco, from Picasso's Pink Period (in room 9; also called *Retrato de la señora Canals*), and then on to the beginnings of cubism. Though the Museu Picasso is no showcase for his cubist period, it does hold a few examples; check out the 1924 *Copa y paquete de tabaco* (Glass and Tobacco Packet) still-life painting (in room 11), a beautiful and simple work that marks the beginning of his fascination with still life.

Las Meninas Through the Prism of Picasso

From 1954 to 1962, Picasso was obsessed with the idea of researching and 'rediscovering' the greats, in particular Velázquez. In 1957 he made a series of renditions of Velázquez' masterpiece *Las meninas* (The Ladies-in-Waiting), now displayed in rooms 12 to 14. It is as though Picasso has looked at the original Velázquez painting through a prism reflecting all the styles he had worked through until then, creating his own masterpiece in the process. This is a wonderful opportunity to see *Las meninas* in its entirety, in a beautiful space.

Getting Around the Collection

The permanent collection is housed in the Palau Aguilar, Palau del Baró de Castellet and Palau Meca, all dating to the 14th century. The 18th-century Casa Mauri, built over medieval remains (even some Roman leftovers have been identified), and the adjacent 14th-century Palau Finestres, accommodate temporary exhibitions.

Ceramics

What is also special about the Museu Picasso is its showcasing of his work in lesser-known media. The last rooms contain Picasso's engravings and 42 ceramic pieces completed throughout the latter years of his unceasingly creative life. You'll see plates and bowls decorated with simple, single-line drawings of fish, owls and other animal shapes, typical for Picasso's daubing on clay. Room 16, meanwhile, displays portraits of Jacqueline from the 1960s.

Top Experience 📷

Step into Basílica de Santa Maria del Mar

At the southwestern end of Passeig del Born is Barcelona's finest Catalan Gothic church, Santa Maria del Mar (Our Lady of the Sea). Begun in 1329, under the watch of architects Berenguer de Montagut and Ramon Despuig, the church is remarkable for its architectural harmony and simplicity. Famously, parishioners gave up their time to help construct the church, particularly the local stevedores.

◎ MAP P82, E5

📞 93 310 23 90; www. santamariadelmar barcelona.org

Plaça de Santa Maria del Mar

🕑 9am-8.30pm Mon-Sat, 10am-8pm Sun

Main Sanctuary

The pleasing unity of form and symmetry of the central nave and two flanking aisles owe much to the rapidity with which the church was built – a mere, record-breaking 54 years. The slender, octagonal pillars create an enormous sense of lateral space, bathed in the light of stained glass. The walls, side chapels and facades were finished by 1350 and the entire structure was completed in 1383.

Ceiling & Side Chapels

Even before anarchists gutted the church in 1909 and again in 1936 (when it famously burned for 11 days straight), Santa Maria always lacked superfluous decoration. Gone are the gilded chapels that weigh heavily over so many Spanish churches, while the splashes of colour high above the nave are subtle – unusually and beautifully so. It all serves to highlight the church's fine proportions, purity of line and sense of space.

The Porters

During the construction, the city's *bastaixos* (porters) spent a day each week carrying across the stone required to build the church from royal quarries in Montjuïc. Their memory lives on in reliefs of them in the main doors and stone carvings elsewhere in the church, a reminder that Santa Maria was conceived as a people's church.

Tours

From 1pm to 5pm (and 2pm to 5pm on Sundays), visitors must pay to enter and join a guided tour (€10), which takes in the main church, galleries and crypt. A separate tour zips you up to the towers and rooftop (€8.50). Musical performances occasionally take place; check the website or ask locally.

★ Top Tips

∘ Take a guided tour (1pm to 5pm) to visit the roof terrace.

∘ If your purpose is spiritual, try to be here for the daily mass at 7.30pm.

∘ Enquire in the gift shop as to whether evening baroque music recitals are scheduled.

✕ Take a Break

Admire the western facade of the church while enjoying tapas and Catalan wines at one of the outdoor tables of La Vinya del Senyor (p81).

Or pop around to Euskal Etxea (p81) for a feast of Basque *pintxos*.

★ Getting There

Ⓜ Jaume I

La Ribera & El Born Basílica de Santa Maria del Mar

Walking Tour 🥾

Tapas & Bar-Hopping in El Born

If there's one place that snapshots all that's irresistible about this city, it has to be El Born, the tangle of streets surrounding the Basílica de Santa Maria del Mar and Passeig del Born, one of the prettiest little boulevards in Spain. This is where barcelonins and local expats go for a real-deal Barcelona night out.

Walk Facts

Start La Vinya del Senyor;
Ⓜ Jaume I

End Bar Sauvage;
Ⓜ Jaume I

Distance 1.5km; four to five hours

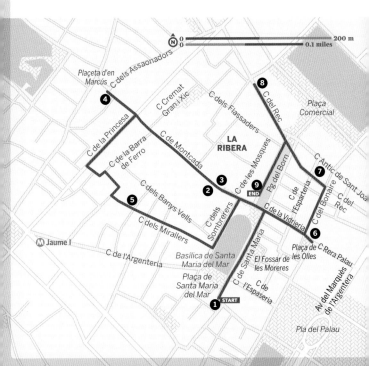

❶ La Vinya del Senyor

Start with Catalan wines at elegant **La Vinya del Senyor** (📞 93 310 33 79; www.facebook.com/vinyadelsenyor; Plaça de Santa Maria del Mar 5; ⏰ noon-1am Sun-Thu, to 2am Fri & Sat; 📶; Ⓜ Jaume I), opposite the Basílica.

❷ El Xampanyet

Wander along Passeig del Born for *cava* (sparkling wine) and home-cooked tapas at **El Xampanyet** (📞 93 319 70 03; www.elxampanyet.es; Carrer de Montcada 22; ⏰ noon-3.30pm & 7-11pm Tue-Sat, noon-3.30pm Sun; 📶; Ⓜ Jaume I).

❸ Euskal Etxea

Next up: the drool-worthy *pintxos* (Basque tapas) at stone-walled **Euskal Etxea** (📞 93 310 21 85; www.gruposagardi.com; Placeta de Montcada 1-3; pintxos €2, mains €12-26; ⏰ bar 10am-12.30am Sun-Thu, to 1am Fri & Sat, restaurant 1-4pm & 7pm-midnight; 📶; Ⓜ Jaume I) – from prawns topped with peppers to deep-fried goat's cheese.

❹ Bar del Pla

Detour to buzzy **Bar del Pla** (📞 93 268 30 03; www.bardelpla.cat; Carrer de Montcada 2; tapas €4-11, mains €9-15; ⏰ noon-11pm Mon-Thu, to midnight Fri & Sat; 📶; Ⓜ Jaume I) for original tapas like wasabi mushrooms.

❺ Dr Stravinsky

Meander back south to experi-mental **Dr Stravinsky** (📞 93 157 12 33; www.drstravinsky.cat; Carrer dels Mirallers 5; ⏰ 6pm-2.30am; Ⓜ Jaume I) for knockout cocktails using homemade ingredients.

❻ Cal Pep

Boisterous **Cal Pep** (📞 93 310 79 61; www.calpep.com; Plaça de les Olles 8; mains €10-20; ⏰ 7.30-11.30pm Mon, 1-3.45pm & 7.30-11.30pm Tue-Sat, closed last 3 weeks Aug; Ⓜ Barcelo-neta) offers some of Barcelona's tastiest seafood tapas such as *cloïsses amb pernil* (clams and ham).

❼ Farola

From soulful jazz to foot-stomping flamenco, live music meets expert-ly crafted cocktails at lively **Farola** (📞 663 332 643; www.farolabcn.com; Carrer del Rec 67; ⏰ 6pm-2.30am Sun-Thu, to 3.30am Fri & Sat).

❽ Bormuth

Zip over to **Bormuth** (📞 93 310 21 86; www.facebook.com/bormuthbar celona; Carrer del Rec 31; tapas €5-10; ⏰ 12.30pm-1.30am Sun-Thu, to 2am Fri & Sat; 📶; Ⓜ Jaume I) for home-made vermouth, Catalan wines and bubbly *cava*.

❾ Bar Sauvage

Party-style **Bar Sauvage** (📞 93 832 51 84; www.barsauvage.com; Passeig del Born 13; ⏰ 7pm-3am; Ⓜ Jaume I) spotlights Latin American spirits (€10 to €12) and Peruvian-Mexican street food.

La Ribera & El Born

Ronda de Sant Pere

1

C del Bruc

C de Trafalgar

Ptge de Sert

C de Trafalgar

C d'Ortigosa

2

C de Méndez Núñez

C de Trafalgar

19

10 🍴

C de Sant Pere més Alt

C d'en Mònec

Palau de la Música Catalana

3

C Palau de la Música

1 ◉

C de Verdaguer i Callís

24 🍴

C de Mare de Deu del Pilar

C de Sant Pere Mitjà

C de Sant Pere més Baix

C de Llúria

el Prado

29 🔒

Monestir de Sant Pere de les Puelles

Plaça de Sant Pere

16 🍴

14 🍴

11 🍴

C del Rec Comtal

C d'en Cortines

Plaça de Comerç

C de les Basses de Sant Pere

C del Portal Nou

C dels Metges

Plaça del Pou de la Figuera

C d'en Llàstics

C de Jaume Giralt

LA RIBERA

C d'en Giralt i Pellisser

Plaça de Sant Agustí Vell

17 🍴

C d'en Tantarantana

C d'Allada Vermell

15 🔒

C del Fonollar

C dels Carders

Via Laietana

C del Dr Joaquim Pou

4

2 ◉

Mercat de Santa Caterina

13 🍴

C de Francesc Cambó

C de les Freixures

C de Colomines

C dels Corders

C dels Assaonadors

C de Montcada

Museu Picasso ◉

Plaça d'Antoni Maura

C dels Mercaders

Av de Francesc Cambó

Museu de Cultures del Món 6 ◉

C dels Banys Vells

Carrer de Montcada

30 🔒

28 🔒

Av de la Catedral

Plaça de la Seu

BARRI GÒTIC

C de la Tapineria

Plaça de Ramon Berenguer el Gran

C de la Bòria

C de la Princesa

9 🍴

C de Grunyí

21 🔒

C Vigatans

C dels Mirallers

C de la Brosolí

27 🔒

5

Plaça Nova

Plaça de l'Àngel

M Jaume I

C de Jaume I

C de Manresa

C de l'Argenteria

Via Laietana

C de la Nau

C de la Basea

C dels Abaixadors

C dels Sots-Tinent Navarro

6

C dels Lledó

C de la Pau

26 🔒

C dels Agullers

For reviews see

◉ Top Experiences p74
◉ Sights p84
🍴 Eating p85
🍷 Drinking p88
🔒 Shopping p90

Ⓝ 0 — 200 m
0 — 0.1 miles

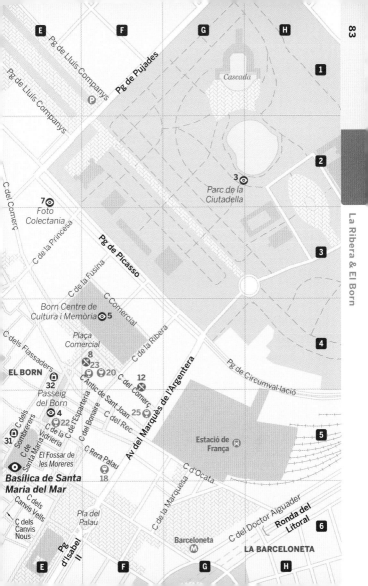

La Ribera & El Born

Pg de Lluís Companys

Pg de Pujades

Pg de Lluís Companys

E **F** **G** **H**

1

Cascada

2

3 ◉

Parc de la Ciutadella

C del Comerç

7 ◉
Foto
Colectania

C de la Princesa

Pg de Picasso

3

C de la Fusina

C Comercial

Born Centre de
Cultura i Memòria ◉ **5**

C dels Flassaders

Plaça
Comercial

C de la Ribera

4

8 ◉
◉ **23**
◉ **20**

EL BORN 🔒
32

C Antic de Sant Joan

C del Comerç

12 ◉

Pg de Circumval·lació

Passeig
del Born

◉ **4**

C de l'Esparteria

C del Bonaire

C del Rec

◉ **25**

Av del Marquès de l'Argentera

31 🔒

C dels Sombrerers

◉ **22**

C de la Vidrieria

C de
Santa Maria

El Fossar de
les Moreres

C Rera Palau

◉ **18**

Estació de
França 🚉

◉
**Basílica de Santa
Maria del Mar**

C d'Ocata

5

C dels
Canvis Vells

Pla del
Palau

C de la Marquesa

C dels
Canvis
Nous

Pg d'Isabel II

Barceloneta Ⓜ

C del Doctor Aiguader

**Ronda del
Litoral**

6

LA BARCELONETA

E **F** **G** **H**

Sights

Palau de la Música Catalana
ARCHITECTURE

1 MAP P82, A3

A fantastical symphony in tile, brick, sculpted stone and stained glass, this Unesco-listed, 2146-seat concert hall is a high point of Barcelona's Modernista architecture. Built by Domènech i Montaner, with the help of some of the best Catalan artisans of the time, between 1905 and 1908, for the Orfeo Català musical society, it was conceived as a temple for the Catalan Renaixença (Renaissance). (☎93 295 72 00; www.palaumusica.cat; Carrer Palau de la Música 4-6; adult/concession/under 10yr €20/16/free; ⏱guided tours 10am-3.30pm Sep-Jun, to 6pm Easter & Jul, 9am-6pm Aug; Ⓜ Urquinaona)

Mercat de Santa Caterina
MARKET

2 ⊙ MAP P82, C3

Come shopping for your tomatoes or pop in for lunch at this extraordinary-looking produce market, designed by forward-thinking architects Enric Miralles and Benedetta Tagliabue to replace its 19th-century predecessor. Completed in 2005 (sadly after Miralles' death in 2000), it's distinguished by its undulating, kaleidoscopic roof, suspended above bustling produce stands, restaurants, cafes and bars by twisting slender branches of what look like grey steel trees. (☎93 319 57 40; www.mercatsantacaterina.com; Avinguda de Francesc Cambó 16; admission free; ⏱7.30am-3.30pm Mon, Wed & Sat, to 8.30pm Tue, Thu & Fri, closed afternoons except Fri Aug; Ⓜ Jaume I)

Parc de la Ciutadella
PARK

3 ⊙ MAP P82, G2

Come for a stroll, a picnic, a lake boat ride, a tour of Catalonia's parliament or to marvel at the swirling waterfall-fountain in which Gaudí had a hand. This is the city's most central green lung, born in the mid-19th century on the former site of the much-hated huge fortress (La Ciutadella) on the eastern side of La Ribera. (Passeig de Picasso; ⏱10am-10.30pm; ⛹; Ⓜ Arc de Triomf)

Passeig del Born
STREET

4 ⊙ MAP P82, E5

Framed by the majestic Basílica de Santa Maria del Mar and the former Mercat del Born, leafy Passeig del Born was Barcelona's main playground from the 13th to 18th centuries. (Ⓜ Barceloneta, Jaume I)

Born Centre de Cultura i Memòria
HISTORIC BUILDING

5 ⊙ MAP P82, F4

Launched in 2013 as part of the events held for the tercentenary of the Catalan defeat in the War of the Spanish Succession, this cultural space is housed in the former

Mercat del Born, a handsome 19th-century structure of slatted iron and brick designed by Josep Fontserè. Excavations in 2001 unearthed remains of whole streets (now exposed on the subterranean level) flattened to make way for the much-hated Ciutadella (citadel), with some sections dating back to Roman and Islamic times. (🖉93 256 68 51; http://elborncultura imemoria.barcelona.cat; Plaça Comercial 12; centre free, exhibition adult/concession/child under 16yr €4.50/3.15/free; ⏰10am-8pm Tue-Sun; Ⓜ Jaume I)

Museu de Cultures del Món
MUSEUM

6 ◉ MAP P82, D4

Opening through a grand courtyard overlooked by an 18th-century staircase, the medieval Palau Nadal and the Palau Marquès de Lió host Barcelona's world cultures museum. Exhibits from private and public collections, including many from Montjuïc's Museu Etnològic (p160), travel through the ancient cultures of Africa, Asia, the Americas and Oceania. (🖉93 256 23 00; http://museuculturesmon.bcn.cat; Carrer de Montcada 12; adult/concession/under 16yr €5/3.50/free, 3-8pm Sun & 1st Sun of month free; ⏰10am-7pm Tue-Sat, to 8pm Sun; Ⓜ Jaume I)

Foto Colectania
GALLERY

7 ◉ MAP P82, E2

Photography lovers should swing by this minimalist-design nonprofit foundation in El Born, which hosts thought-provoking, regularly changing exhibitions from across the globe and also works to bring Catalan and Spanish photography to the world. (🖉93 217 16 26; http://fotocolectania.org; Passeig de Picasso 14; adult/concession/child under 14yr €4/3/free, 1st Sun of month free; ⏰11am-8pm Tue-Sat, to 3pm Sun; Ⓜ Arc de Triomf, Jaume I)

Eating

Casa Delfín
CATALAN €€

8 🍴 MAP P82, F4

One of El Born's culinary delights, Casa Delfín is everything you might dream about Catalan-Mediterranean cooking in a traditional style. It's lined with wine bottles inside, the service is spot-on and creative presentation lends a contemporary touch. Menus change depending on market produce, but might offer salt-strewn *Padrón* peppers, plump anchovies from L'Escala, big seafood paellas or *suquet dels pescadors* (Catalan fish stew) for two. (🖉93 319 50 88; www.casadelfinrestaurant.com; Passeig del Born 36; tapas €6-11, mains €12-20; ⏰noon-midnight Sun-Thu, to 1am Fri & Sat; 📶; Ⓜ Jaume I)

Can Cisa/Bar Brutal
SPANISH €€

9 🍴 MAP P82, C5

Can Cisa's elegant all-natural wines pair beautifully with Bar Brutal's innovative reimagining of fresh Catalan ingredients at this rowdy, fashionable wine-bar-restaurant venture from Barcelona culinary

Carrer de Montcada

Today running between the Romanesque Capella d'en Marcús and Passeig del Born, this medieval **high street** (M Jaume I) was driven towards the sea from the road that in the 12th century led northeast from the city walls. It became Barcelona's most coveted address for the merchant classes; the great mansions that remain today mostly date from the 14th and 15th centuries.

kings the Colombo brothers and team. Straight from the open kitchen, octopus with pak choi, watermelon-tomato salad and delicate artisan cheeses pull in a young, fun crowd until late. Wines are sourced from across Spain, Italy and France. (📞93 295 47 97, 93 319 98 81; www.cancisa.cat; Carrer de la Princesa 14; mains €11-20; ⏰7pm-1.30am Mon, 1-4pm & 7pm-2am Tue-Thu, 1pm-2am Fri & Sat Oct-Jun, 7pm-2am Mon-Thu, 1pm-2am Fri & Sat Jul-Sep; M Jaume I)

Casa Lolea   TAPAS €

10 MAP P82, B2

Dangling strings of tomatoes and garlic, red-and-black-spot decor and whitewashed brick walls lend an air of Andalucian charm to this cheerful tapas-and-vermouth tavern. It's popular for its lightly creative breakfast *entrepans* (sandwiches) and classic-with-

a-twist tapas such as mushroom scrambles, just-cooked tortilla and platters of northern Spanish cheeses and cured ham. (📞93 624 10 16; www.casalolea.com; Carrer de Sant Pere més Alt 49; tapas €4-14; ⏰9am-1am; 📶)

Fismuler   MEDITERRANEAN €€€

11 MAP P82, D1

The brainchild of three ex El Bulli chefs, the minimalist-design Barcelona outpost of this Madrid-born market-based sensation is one of the city's hottest tickets. Daily-changing menus throw seasonal local produce into expertly executed, unpretentious Spanish–Mediterranean dishes: Delta de l'Ebre oysters, cod omelette, truffle-and-burrata salad or slow-cooked fennel seabass, followed by gooey cheesecake and with Catalan wines to start. (📞93 514 00 50; www.fismuler.com; Carrer del Rec Comtal 17; tapas €4-17, mains €20-25; ⏰1.30-4pm & 8-11pm Sun-Wed, to 11.30pm Thu-Sat; 🍴; M Arc de Triomf)

Koku Kitchen Buns   ASIAN €

12 MAP P82, F4

A stylish brick-walled space with scattered plants and communal tables, Koku serves delectable homemade bao stuffed with beef, pork or tofu, as well as dumplings, Vietnamese pho and fresh lemonade, sourcing most ingredients locally. The basement ramen-and-gyoza bar (closed lunch June to August) offers some of Barcelona's best steaming noodle bowls.

On weekdays there's a great-value lunch *menú* (€13.50). (☏ 93 269 65 36; www.kokukitchen.es; Carrer del Comerç 29; mains €9-11; ⏱ 1-4pm & 7.30-11.30pm; 🛜 🍴; Ⓜ Barceloneta)

Bar Joan CATALAN €

13 🍴 MAP P82, C3

A locally popular stop inside the Mercat de Santa Caterina (p84), old-school Bar Joan is known especially for its *arròs negre* (cuttlefish-ink rice) on Tuesdays and paella on Thursdays. It's a simple, friendly and good-value spot, serving only tapas, *entrepans* (filled rolls) or the excellent-value *menú del dia*, with plenty of choice. (☏ 93 310 61 50; Avinguda de Francesc Cambó 16, Mercat de Santa Caterina; menú del dia €12.50, tapas €3-5; ⏱ 7.30am-3.30pm Mon, Wed & Sat, to 5pm Tue, Thu & Fri; 🛜; Ⓜ Jaume I)

Nakashita JAPANESE €€

14 🍴 MAP P82, D1

Brazil's particular immigration story means it has a tradition of superb Japanese food, and the Brazilian chef at Nakashita is no slouch, turning out excellent sashimi, maki rolls, softshell crab and *kakiage* (a mix of tempura). It's one of the top Japanese restaurants in Barcelona, with just a handful of tables – book if you can. (☏ 93 295 53 78; www.nakashitabcn.com; Carrer del Rec Comtal 15; mains €10-22; ⏱ 1-4pm & 8pm-midnight; 🛜; Ⓜ Arc de Triomf)

Tantarantana MEDITERRANEAN €

15 🍴 MAP P82, D3

All patterned tiled floors, marble-top tables and wooden beams, shoebox-sized Tantarantana attracts a lively crowd who make the most of the terrace tables in warmer months. Well-prepared, market-driven Mediterranean dishes and tapas swing from wild-mushroom risotto and citrusy deep-fried aubergines to cod with ratatouille. The lemon-meringue cake is divine. (☏ 93 268 24 10; www.gruposantelmo.com; Carrer d'en Tantarantana 24; tapas €5-10, mains €9-12; ⏱ 1pm-midnight; 🛜; Ⓜ Jaume I)

Elsa y Fred INTERNATIONAL €

16 🍴 MAP P82, C1

Named after an Argentinean film, Elsa y Fred feels like a cosy, old-school-glam living room, with a wooden fireplace, mirrored pillars and sink-down leather armchairs. The menu features gourmet tapas such as mandarin and orange salad with goat's cheese or grilled baby squid with yuzu emulsion. There's a €14.50 weekday set lunch, plus cakes, cocktails and weekend brunch (until 4pm!). (☏ 93 501 66 11; www.elsayfred.es; Carrer del Rec Comtal 11; tapas & brunch €4-10; ⏱ 8.30am-midnight Mon-Fri, from 9am Sat & Sun; 🛜 🍴; Ⓜ Arc de Triomf)

Mosquito ASIAN €

17 🍴 MAP P82, D3

This pint-sized, always-busy, unadorned spot is devoted to great-value 'Asian tapas'. Local Catalan ingredients are worked into fragrant Vietnamese pho, salted edamame, Chinese dim sum, Japanese gyoza and the like, accompanied by craft beers or teas from Barcelona emporium Čaj Chai (📞 93 301 95 92; www.cajchai.com; Carrer de Salomó Ben Adret 12; ⏰ 10.30am-10pm Thu-Mon; Ⓜ Jaume I). No bookings. (📞 93 268 75 69; www.mosquitotapas.com; Carrer dels Carders 46; dishes €3-6; ⏰ 7-11pm Mon, 1-5pm & 7-11pm Tue-Sun)

Espai Mescladís MEDITERRANEAN €

Rainbow-coloured chairs and tables sit under medieval stone arches at this nonprofit social-project cafe-bar (just down the road from Mosquito), which helps integrate immigrants to Barcelona. The North African–Mediterranean menu swings from hummus, tabbouleh and tagines to *patates braves* and zingy fresh lemonade, and there's a good value €12 set lunch on week-days. (📞 93 319 87 32; www.facebook.com/mescladis; Carrer dels Carders 35; dishes €3-8; ⏰ 10am-8.30pm; 🍴)

Drinking

Paradiso/Pastrami Bar COCKTAIL BAR

18 🍸 MAP P82, F5

A kind of Narnia-in-reverse, Paradiso is fronted by a snowy-white wardrobe-sized space, with pastrami sandwiches, pulled pork and other home-cured delights. But this is only the portal – step through the fridge door into a glam, sexy speakeasy guaranteed to raise the most world-weary of eyebrows, where highly creative, artfully prepared cocktails (€9 to €12) steal the show. Worth queue-ing for. (📞 639 310671; www.paradiso.cat; Carrer de Rera Palau 4; ⏰ 7pm-1.15am Sun-Thu, to 2.15am Fri & Sat; 🛜; Ⓜ Barceloneta)

Nømad Cøffee Lab & Shop COFFEE

19 ☕ MAP P82, B1

King of Barcelona's third-wave coffee scene, Nømad is known for its seasonally sourced, small-batch, Barcelona-roasted beans and experimental techniques. Owner and barista Jordi Mestre was inspired by his time in London and, at this snug, minimalist, lab-style cafe, it's all about coffee tastings and expertly poured espresso, flat whites, cold brews and Aeropress (€2 to €5). (📞 628 566235; www.nomadcoffee.es; Passatge de Sert 12; ⏰ 8.30am-5pm Mon-Fri; Ⓜ Urquinaona)

Guzzo COCKTAIL BAR

20 🍸 MAP P82, F4

With good vibes anytime of day, this old-school cocktail bar is run by much-loved Barcelona DJ Fred Guzzo, who is often at the decks spinning his delicious selection of funk, soul and rare groove. You'll also find frequent live-music acts, excellent mojitos (€8) and tasty homemade tapas like burrata fresh from Santa Caterina market. (📞93 667 00 36; www.guzzorestau rante.es; Plaça Comercial 10; ⏰7-11.30pm Mon-Fri, 1-4pm & 7-11.30pm Sat & Sun; 🛜; Ⓜ Jaume I)

Mag by El Magnífico   COFFEE

21 Ⓟ MAP P82, D5

One of Barcelona's best coffee roasters, El Magnífico (p90) now runs this stylish, Scandi-esque corner cafe breathing new life into a beautiful 19th-century building with wooden beams, Catalan arched ceilings, original stained glass and huge roasting machines. Pair your freshly roasted, seasonally sourced blends espresso (€2) with decadent flaky pastries from the nearby Hofmann Pastisseria (p91). (📞93 488 57 86; www.face book.com/magbyelmagnifico; Carrer de Grunyí 10; ⏰10am-6pm Fri-Sun; Ⓜ Jaume I)

Creps al Born   COCKTAIL BAR

22 Ⓟ MAP P82, E5

A rowdy, jam-packed and seriously fun party-loving cocktail bar, where people spill out onto Passeig del Born over wildly creative artisan cocktails (€10 to €12) and popular mojitos. Good crepes, too. (📞93 269 03 25; www.facebook.com/Crep salBorn; Passeig del Born 12; ⏰6pm-3am Mon-Fri, noon-4am Sat, noon-2am Sun; Ⓜ Jaume I)

El Diset   WINE BAR

23 Ⓟ MAP P82, F4

Dealing almost exclusively in Catalan drops, El Diset is a sleek, candlelit wine, cocktail and tapas bar that also does tastings. Thin *torrades* (toasted bread) topped with, say, goat's cheese and stir-fried vegetables or tuna tataki and tapas of Catalan cheeses accompany glasses (€4 to €7) of Terra Alta, Montsant, Penedès, Priorat and more. (📞93 268 19 87; www. facebook.com/eldiset; Carrer Antic de Sant Joan 3; ⏰7pm-2am Mon-Thu, to 3am Fri, 1pm-3am Sat, 1pm-2am Sun; Ⓜ Barceloneta,)

Bar de l'Antic Teatre   BAR

24 Ⓟ MAP P82, A3

There's often a queue for tables on the buzzy boho garden terrace at this relaxed community cafe-bar. It's set in the shade of a fig tree hidden away in a 17th-century building, down an alley opposite the Palau de la Música Catalana. Perfect for morning coffee, or beers and wine (€3) later on. (📞93 315 23 54; www.anticteatre.com; Carrer Verdaguer i Callís 12; ⏰10am-11.30pm Mon-Thu, to midnight Fri, 5pm-midnight Sat, 5-11.30pm Sun; 🛜; Ⓜ Urquinaona)

Clubhaus   BAR

25 Ⓟ MAP P82, F5

Upstairs: graffiti-clad concrete walls, a lively pool table, Mexican-style street food. Downstairs: table

Casa Gispert

tennis, crafted cocktails, meaty American-inspired snacks, DJs from 11pm. Overall, artsy multi-concept 2019 arrival Clubhaus keeps up the pace from coffee to brunch to espresso martinis and late-night karaoke. The food focus is on homemade ingredients and a low-plastic ethos; local artists' work is also on display. (☎93 858 84 66; www.clubhaus.es; Avinguda del Marquès de l'Argentera 13; ⏰6pm-2.30am Mon-Thu, 5pm-3am Fri, 1pm-3am Sat, 1pm-2.30am Sun; Ⓜ Barceloneta)

Shopping

Vila Viniteca FOOD & DRINKS

26 🔒 MAP P82, D6

One of Barcelona's best wine stores (and there are a few...), Vila Viniteca has been hunting down the finest local and imported wines since 1932. There are year-round on-request tastings and a handful of bar tables, and on several November evenings it organises an almost riotous wine-tasting event at which cellars from across Spain present their young new wines. (www.vilaviniteca. es; Carrer dels Agullers 7; ⏰8.30am-8.30pm Mon-Sat; Ⓜ Jaume I)

El Magnífico COFFEE

27 🔒 MAP P82, D5

All sorts of coffee beans, sourced seasonally from around the world, have been roasted at much-loved third-generation family-owned El Magnífico (which you'll spot all over town) since the early 20th century – and the aromas hit as soon as you walk in. Sample a cup on-site or wander over to the sleek Mag cafe (p89) on nearby Carrer de Grunyí. (www.cafeselmag nifico.com; Carrer de l'Argenteria 64; ⏰10am-8pm Mon-Sat; Ⓜ Jaume I)

Capsule FASHION & ACCESSORIES

28 🔒 MAP P82, D5

Elegantly understated fashion and homewares sourced from small, sustainable, independent Spanish and international brands grace this tucked-away boutique. Capsule occupies a reimagined brick-walled stable, and spot-lights female artisans working with traditional techniques and organic materials. (www.capsule bcn.com; Carrer dels Banys Vells 21;

HANS GEEL/SHUTTERSTOCK ©

⊙noon-8pm Tue-Sat; Ⓜ Jaume I, Barceloneta)

Working in the Redwoods
CERAMICS

29 🔒 MAP P82, C1

Catalan designer Miriam Cornuda handcrafts beautiful, minimalist, earthy-toned bowls, mugs, vases and other ceramics from all-natural materials, inspired by the colours of the Costa Brava, at this soothing studio-workshop near the Arc de Triomf. There are also occasional ceramics classes (check online). (📞 93 301 66 63; www.workingintheredwoods.com; Carrer de Lluís el Piadós 4; ⊙noon-8pm Mon-Sat; Ⓜ Arc de Triomf)

Ozz Barcelona
FASHION & ACCESSORIES

30 🔒 MAP P82, D5

Cutting-edge Barcelona designers take centre stage at slow-fashion-focused concept boutique and coworking space Ozz. Its handmade jewellery and bold clothing come courtesy of emerging, independent brands such as Txell Miras, IKA, Ester Gueroa and Antonio Rodríguez. (📞 93 315 84 81; www.ozzbarcelona.com; Carrer dels Banys Vells 8; ⊙10.30am-9pm; Ⓜ Jaume I)

Casa Gispert
FOOD

31 🔒 MAP P82, E5

Wonderful, atmospheric, wood-fronted Casa Gispert has been toasting nuts and selling all manner of dried fruit since 1851. Pots and jars piled high on the shelves contain an unending variety of crunchy titbits: some roasted, some honeyed, all of them moreish. (📞 93 319 75 35; www.casagispert.com; Carrer dels Sombrerers 23; ⊙10am-8.30pm Mon-Sat; Ⓜ Jaume I)

Hofmann Pastisseria
FOOD

32 🔒 MAP P82, E4

All painted wooden cabinets and Tiffany-blue interiors, this bite-sized gourmet patisserie is linked to the prestigious Hofmann cooking school. Choose between jars of delicious jams, the prize-winning mascarpone-filled croissants (also in other flavours!) and more dangerous pastries, or an array of cakes and other sweet treats. Hofmann also has a cafe a few doors down. (📞 93 268 82 21; www.hofmann-bcn.com; Carrer dels Flassaders 44; ⊙9am-2pm & 3.30-8pm Mon-Sat, 9am-2pm Sun; Ⓜ Barceloneta, Jaume I)

Explore ⊕

Barceloneta, the Waterfront & El Poblenou

Dramatically transformed since the 20th century, Barcelona's formerly industrial waterfront now boasts sparkling beaches, ultramodern high-rises, yacht-filled marinas and a lovely seaside promenade. The gateway to the Mediterranean is the old-fashioned fishing quarter of Barceloneta, filled with seafood restaurants. To the northeast, post-industrial El Poblenou has creative design spaces and popular beaches.

The Short List

○ **El Poblenou Platges (p98)** *Basking on these sun-kissed sandy beaches, before a dip in the glittering Mediterranean and a xiringuito lunch.*

○ **Barceloneta Dining (p95)** *Hopping between this seaside barri's down-to-earth tapas bars (don't miss La Cova Fumada), or hunting down the perfect paella.*

○ **Design in El Poblenou (p100)** *Wandering between creative cafes, forward-thinking boutiques and ambitious arts projects such as Espacio 88 in this up-and-coming, formerly industrial neighbourhood.*

○ **Museu d'Història de Catalunya (p98)** *Learning about the Romans, Moors, feudal lords and civil war freedom fighters, followed by drinks at the rooftop restaurant.*

Getting There & Around

Ⓜ Go to Drassanes (Línia 3) to reach Port Vell; Barceloneta (Línia 4) has its own stop. Línia 4 continues out to Ciutadella Vila Olímpica, El Poblenou and El Maresme Fòrum.

Neighbourhood Map on p96

W Barcelona hotel ARCHITECT: RICARDO BOFILL. LENA SERDITOVA/SHUTTERSTOCK©

Walking Tour 🥾

Barceloneta: Sea & Seafood

Barcelona's Mediterranean roots are nowhere more pronounced than in sunny Barceloneta, a seaside peninsula with a salty air and an enduring relationship with the sea. As often as not, this is one area where locals outnumber tourists, at least on weekends when the city's restaurants and beaches throng with a predominantly local crowd.

Walk Facts

Start Can Paixano; Ⓜ Barceloneta

End Port Olímpic; Ⓜ Ciutadella Vila Olímpica

Length 2.5km; as long as you like!

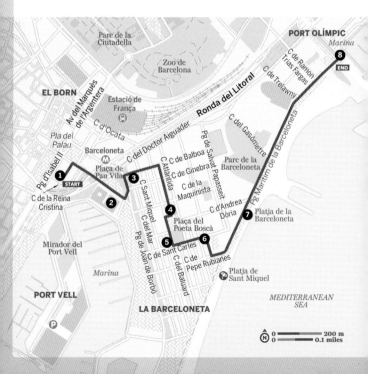

❶ Can Paixano

It doesn't come any more authentic than **Can Paixano** (La Xampanyeria; 📞93 310 08 39; www.canpaixano.com; Carrer de la Reina Cristina 7; 🕙9am-10.30pm Mon-Sat; Ⓜ Barceloneta), one of Barcelona's best old-style *cava* (sparkling wine) bars. It's loved for its bubbly rosé, combined with bite-sized *entrepans* (filled rolls) and tapas.

❷ 1881

Head to the top floor of the Museu d'Història de Catalunya to elegant terrace bar-restaurant **1881** (📞93 221 00 50; www.gruposagardi.com; Plaça de Pau Vila 3; mains €18-35; 🕙10am-midnight; 🖊; Ⓜ Barceloneta). *Txuletón* (aged Basque beef) and fresh seafood are specialities.

❸ Vaso de Oro

Always packed, old-school **Vaso de Oro** (📞93 319 30 98; www.vasodeoro.com; Carrer de Balboa 6; tapas €3-10; 🕙11am-midnight, closed 3 weeks Sep; Ⓜ Barceloneta) gathers a high-spirited crowd for fantastic tapas: grilled *gambes* (prawns), *patates amanides* (Andalucian-style potato salad), *solomillo* (sirloin) chunks.

❹ Mercat de la Barceloneta

Barceloneta's **market** (Plaça del Poeta Boscà 1-2; 🕙7am-2pm Mon-Thu, to 8pm Fri, to 3pm Sat; Ⓜ Barceloneta) has seasonal produce, seafood stalls and sit-down restaurants. Don't miss Baluard Barceloneta opposite, one of the city's best bakeries.

❺ La Cova Fumada

Tiny, frills-free, family-run **La Cova Fumada** (📞93 221 40 61; Carrer del Baluard 56; tapas €3-12; 🕙9am-3.15pm Mon-Wed, 9am-3.15pm & 6-8.15pm Thu & Fri, 9am-1pm Sat; Ⓜ Barceloneta) is a Barceloneta (and Barcelona) legend. The secret? Mouth-watering octopus, calamari, sardines, grilled *carxofes* (artichokes) and signature *bombes* (meat-and-potato croquettes).

❻ Bar Leo

An almost entirely *barcelonin* crowd spills out into the street from **Bar Leo** (Carrer de Sant Carles 34; 🕙noon-9.30pm; Ⓜ Barceloneta), a hole-in-the-wall drinking den plastered with images of late Andalucian singer Bambino.

❼ Platja de Barceloneta

Golden **Platja de la Barceloneta** (Ⓜ Barceloneta), the beach closest to Barceloneta, is an iconic spot in the world's coolest city – perhaps best first thing or over a sunset stroll.

❽ Port Olímpic

The 1.25km Passeig Marítim de la Barceloneta promenade shadows the waterfront all the way to the busy, restaurant-lined **Port Olímpic marina** (Moll de Mestral; Ⓜ Ciutadella Vila Olímpica).

Barceloneta, the Waterfront & El Poblenou

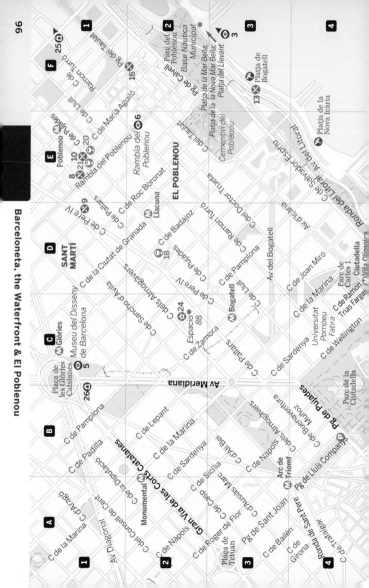

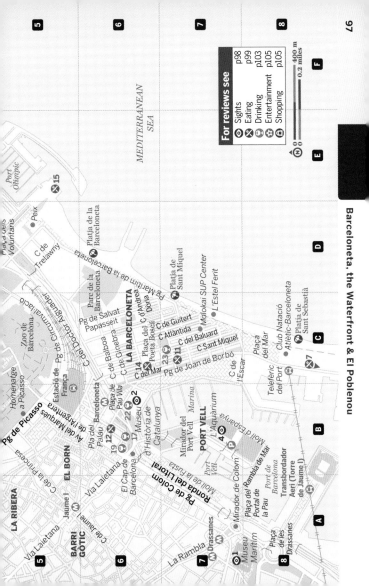

Sights

Museu Marítim

MUSEUM

1 ⊙ MAP P96, A7

The city's maritime museum occupies the mighty Gothic Reials Drassanes (Royal Shipyards) – a remarkable relic from Barcelona's days as the seat of a seafaring empire. Highlights include a full-scale 1970s replica of Don Juan de Austria's 16th-century flagship, fishing vessels, antique navigation charts and dioramas of the Barcelona waterfront. (☑93 342 99 20; www.mmb.cat; Avinguda de les Drassanes; adult/child €10/5, from 3pm Sun free; ⊙10am-8pm; ⓂDrassanes)

Museu d'Història de Catalunya

MUSEUM

2 ⊙ MAP P96, B6

Within the revitalised 1880s **Palau de Mar** (Plaça de Pau Vila; ⓂBarceloneta), this excellent museum travels from the Stone Age through to the arrival of Modernisme in Catalonia and the Spanish Civil War (touching heavily on the cultural and political repression felt across Catalonia postwar) and into the 21st century. It's a busy multimedia hotchpotch of dioramas, artefacts, videos, models, documents and interactive bits. (☑93 225 47 00; www.mhcat.cat; Plaça de Pau Vila 3; adult/child €6/free, 1st Sun of month free; ⊙10am-7pm Tue & Thu-Sat, to 8pm Wed, to 2.30pm Sun; ⓂBarceloneta)

El Poblenou Platges

BEACH

3 ⊙ MAP P96, B6

A series of beautiful, broad, sandy golden beaches dotted with *xiringuitos* (seasonal beach bars) stretches northeast from the Port Olímpic marina. They're largely artificial, but that doesn't deter the millions of sunseekers and swimmers from descending in summer, especially for beach volleyball – and they're still quieter than the sandy strands closer to the city centre. (ⓂCiutadella Vila Olímpica, Llacuna, Poblenou, Selva de Mar)

L'Aquàrium

AQUARIUM

4 ⊙ MAP P96, B7

It's hard not to shudder at the sight of a shark gliding above you, displaying its toothy, wide-mouthed grin – but this 80m shark tunnel is the highlight of one of Europe's largest aquariums. Jutting out into the port, Barcelona's aquarium is home to the world's best Mediterranean collection, as well as plenty of colourful fish from as far off as the Red Sea, the Caribbean and the Great Barrier Reef. A staggering 11,000 creatures of 450 species reside here. (☑93 221 74 74; www.aquariumbcn.com; Moll d'Espanya; adult/child €21/16; ⊙10am-9pm Easter & Jun-Sep, reduced hours Oct-May; ♦; ⓂDrassanes)

Museu del Disseny de Barcelona

MUSEUM

5 ⊙ MAP P96, C1

Nicknamed *la grapadora* (the stapler), Barcelona's fascinating design museum lies inside a monolithic contemporary building with geometric facades and a rather brutalist appearance. Inside, it houses a dazzling collection of ceramics, fashion, decorative arts and textiles. (✆93 256 68 00; www.museudeldisseny.cat; Plaça de les Glòries Catalanes 37; adult/child €6/4, from 3pm Sun & 1st Sun of the month free; ⏰10am-8pm Tue-Sun; Ⓜ Glòries)

Rambla del Poblenou STREET

6 ◉ MAP P96, E2

With its origins in the mid-19th century (when Poblenou's industrial boom kicked off), this leafy boulevard has long been the neighbourhood hub, sprinkled with tapas bars and restaurants, and flanked by a few Modernista buildings.

Eating

La Barra de Carles Abellán SEAFOOD €€€

7 ✗ MAP P96, C8

Star Catalan chef Carles Abellán's stunning glass-encased, glossy-tiled restaurant (designed by favourite local interiorist Lázaro Rosa-Violán) celebrates seafood. Stellar tapas might include pickled octopus and *papas aliñás* (potato salad) with mackerel. Even more show-stopping are the mains: grilled razor clams with *ponzu* citrus sauce, squid filled with spicy poached egg yolk, and hake *kokotxas* (jowls) in a *pil pil* (garlic, chilli and oil) sauce. (✆93 295 26 36; www.carlesabellan.com; Plaça de la Rosa dels Vents 1, W Barcelona; tapas

Museu del Disseny de Barcelona and Torre Glòries

Espacio 88

Hosting everything from yoga classes, pop-up boutiques and brunches to the (permanent) uberpopular SKYE coffee truck, the white-walled, concrete-floored warehouse-like **Espacio 88** (Map p96, C2; ☑93 356 88 18; www.espacio88.com; Carrer de Pamplona 88; ⊙9am-5pm Mon-Fri; Ⓜ Bogatell) embodies all that's wonderful about El Poblenou's post-industrial resurgence. The arts take centre stage in dynamic events and exhibitions.

€5-25, mains €18-36; ⊙7-11am & 7-11.30pm Mon-Thu, 7-11am, 1.30-4pm & 7-11.30pm Fri & Sat, 7-11.30am & 1.30-4pm Sun; ☐V15, V19, Ⓜ Barceloneta)

Can Recasens   CATALAN €€

 8 ⊗ MAP P96, E1

One of El Poblenou's most romantic settings, century-old Can Recasens conceals a warren of warmly lit rooms full of oil paintings, flickering candles, fairy lights and fruit baskets. The food is outstanding, with a mix of salads, smoked meats, fondues, and open sandwiches topped with delicacies such as wild mushrooms and Brie, *escalivada* (grilled vegetables) and Gruyère, or *sobrasada* (spicy cured sausage) with rosemary honey. (☑93 300 81 23; www.canrecasens.restaurant; Rambla del Poblenou 102; mains €8-21;

⊙restaurant 8pm-1am, delicatessen 8.15am-1.30pm & 5pm-1am Mon-Fri, 8.15am-1.30pm Sat; Ⓜ Poblenou)

Little Fern Café   CAFE €

9 ⊗ MAP P96, D1

Worth a trip out to El Poblenou in itself, this beautiful Kiwi-Hungarian-owned cafe epitomises the area's newfound allure. White-brick walls, floor-to-ceiling windows and plants in terracotta pots form the backdrop to firmly original all-day-brunch bites fired by organic ingredients, such as fluffy corn fritters with smashed avocado and beetroot relish. There are also sunny mimosas, Edge Brewing craft beers, and coffee by London-based Ozone. (☑93 808 93 17; www.littleferncafe.com; Carrer de Pere IV; dishes €6-10; ⊙9am-5pm Mon, Thu & Fri, from 10am Sat & Sun; 🛜; Ⓜ Poblenou, Glòries)

Minyam   SEAFOOD €€

10 ⊗ MAP P96, E1

Billowing with smoke beneath a tajine-like metal lid, smouldering herbs infuse the rice of Minyam's signature Vulcanus (smoked seafood paella with squid ink). Tapas dishes at this stylish, contemporary El Poblenou restaurant are equally inventive and include asparagus fritters, oysters with sea urchin and lemon, prawn omelettes and fondue with truffle oil. There's a popular €12.50 *menú del dia*. (☑93 348 36 18; www.facebook.com/minyamcisco; Carrer de Pujades 187; tapas €2-10, mains €15-25; ⊙1-11pm

Tue-Thu, to 11.30pm Fri & Sat, to 5pm Sun; MPoblenou)

Can Solé
SEAFOOD €€€

11 MAP P96, C7

Behind imposing wooden doors, this elegantly old-school restaurant with white cloth tables, white-jacketed waiters and photos of celebrity customers has been serving terrific seafood since 1903. Freshly landed catch stars in traditional dishes such as *arròs caldòs* (rice broth with squid and langoustines) and 'grandmother'-style dishes like *zarzuela* (casserole with ground almonds, saffron, garlic, tomatoes, mussels, fish and white wine). (93 221 50 12; www.restaurantcansole.com; Carrer de Sant Carles 4; mains €15-40; 1-4pm & 8-11pm Tue-Thu, 1-4pm & 8.30-11pm Fri & Sat, 1-4pm Sun; MBarceloneta)

Oaxaca
MEXICAN €€€

12 MAP P96, B6

Menorcan chef Joan Bagur trained in Mexico for a decade under traditional cooks and has his own garden of Mexican plants, which supplies ingredients for outstanding culinary creations such as char-grilled octopus and *cochinita pibil* (slow-roasted pork tacos). Hefty tables are made from Mexican hardwoods, original Mexican art lines the walls and there's alfresco seating under the arches. (93 319 00 64; www.oaxacacuinamexicana.com; Pla de Palau 19; mains €14-28; restaurant 1-4pm & 8pm-midnight, bar 1pm-midnight; ; MBarceloneta)

Waterfront Fun

Molokai SUP Center (Map p96, C7; 93 221 48 68; www.molokaisupcenter.com; Carrer de Meer 39; 2hr private SUP/surf lesson from €40/35, SUP/surf board rental per hour €15/12; 10am-6pm Tue-Sat, to 3pm Sun; MBarceloneta) Paddle or surf out into the Mediterranean.

Club Natació Atlètic-Barceloneta (Map p96, C8; 93 221 00 10; www.cnab.cat; Plaça del Mar; day pass adult/child €13/7.40; 6.30am-11pm Mon-Fri, 7am-11pm Sat, 8am-5pm Sun, to 8pm Sun mid-May–Sep; V15, V19, MBarceloneta) Warm and cool lap pools next to La Barceloneta.

Base Náutica Municipal (Map p96, F2; 93 221 04 32; www.basenautica.org; Avinguda del Litoral, Platja de la Mar Bella; 2hr lessons from €40, equipment hire per hour from €15; 9am-8pm; MPoblenou) Kayaking, windsurfing, kitesurfing, sailing and SUP from Platja de la Mar Bella.

Xiringuito Escribà
SEAFOOD €€€

13 MAP P96, F3

The team behind **Escribà** (p41), which has been creating sweets since 1906, is also in charge of one of Barcelona's most popular waterfront seafood restaurants. A whirl of busy waiters and bubbling paellas, this is one of few places in town that does one-person paella or Catalan *fideuà*, as well as delicious vegetarian-friendly mushroom paella. Reservations recommended. (93 221 07 29; www.xiringuitoescriba.com; Avinguda del Litoral 62; mains €18-26; noon-10.30pm; ; H16, V25, V27, M Llacuna)

Bodega La Peninsular TAPAS €

14 MAP P96, C6

At this traditional-style bodega with marble-topped tables, more than three dozen artfully presented tapas pair with Catalan vintages and house-made vermouth. Adhering to the Slow Food ethos, ingredients are organic, seasonal and locally sourced; try the *mojama* (salt-cured, air-dried tuna), the renowned spicy *bombes*

(meat-and-potato croquettes) with tangy aioli, or a giant wedge of tortilla. (93 221 40 89; www.tabernaycafetin.es; Carrer del Mar 29; tapas €5-10; 11.30am-midnight; M Barceloneta)

Red Fish SEAFOOD €€

15 MAP P96, E5

Bamboo chairs, swaying straw lamps, niftily repurposed paddle-boat tables – this chic beachy seafooder sits on its own tucked-away patch of blonde sand at the northwest end of Platja de la Barceloneta. Utterly fabulous Barcelona panoramas unfold as you tuck into superb, fresh rice dishes (like creamy lobster rice), clams in sherry or grilled turbot, or kick back over mojitos, vermouth and sharing platters. (93 171 68 94; www.redfishbcn.com; Moll de la Marina; tapas €2-12, mains €15-30; M Ciutadella Vila Olímpica)

Els Pescadors SEAFOOD €€€

16 MAP P96, F2

On a picturesque square lined with low houses and long-established South American *bella ombre* trees, this quaint family restaurant continues to serve some of the city's best grilled fish and seafood-and-rice dishes. There are three dining areas inside: two are quite modern, while the main room preserves its old tavern flavour. On warm nights, try for a table outside. (93 225 20 18; www.elspescadors.com; Plaça de Prim 1; mains €15-40; 1-3.30pm & 7.45-11.30pm; ; M Poblenou)

El Cap de Barcelona

El 58

TAPAS €

This French-Catalan fave (see 5 Map p96, C1) serves imaginative, beautifully prepared seasonal tapas: braised tuna with *romesco* sauce and asparagus, fried aubergines with honey and rosemary, sausage-and-chickpea stew, and local cheeses. Solo diners can take a seat at the marble-topped front bar. The back dining room with its exposed-brick walls, industrial light fixtures and original artworks is a lively place to linger over a long meal. (Le cinquante huit; 📞93 601 39 03; www.facebook.com/el58poblenou; Rambla del Poblenou 58; tapas €4-12; ⏱1.30-11pm Tue-Sat, to 4pm Sun; Ⓜ Poblenou)

Drinking

Perikete

WINE BAR

17 Ⓖ MAP P96, B6

Since opening in 2017, this fabulous wine spot has been jam-packed with *barcelonins* and visitors. Jabugo hams hang from the ceiling, vermouth barrels sit above the bar and wine bottles cram every available shelf space. There are more than 200 varieties by the glass or bottle, accompanied by excellent tapas (€4 to €10) such as made-to-order tortilla. (📞93 024 22 29; www.gruporeini.com; Carrer de Llauder 6; ⏱noon-1am; Ⓜ Barceloneta)

Espai Joliu

CAFE

18 Ⓖ MAP P96, D2

Inspired by its owner's time in Berlin, this charmingly stylish

Seaside Sculpture

The waterfront area hosts an array of intriguing street sculpture, most notably **Peix** (Map p96, D5; Carrer de Ramon Trias Fargas 2; Ⓜ Ciutadella Villa Olímpica) , Frank Gehry's shimmering, bronze-coloured headless fish facing the Port Olímpic. Other works include **El Cap de Barcelona** (Map p96, B6; Passeig de Colom; Ⓜ Barceloneta) by Roy Lichtenstein at the Port Vell and Rebecca Horn's 1992 tribute to the old waterfront shacks, **L'Estel Ferit** (Map p96, C7; Passeig Marítim de la Barceloneta; Ⓜ Barceloneta).

former carpenters' workshop is Barcelona's original plants-and-coffee concept cafe (much-copied since). Potted plants, design mags and ceramics are sold up the front, while the peaceful cafe has recycled timber furniture, stone walls and exposed bulbs, and serves Barcelona-roasted Nømad coffee (€2 to €3) and organic cakes (try the gluten-free lemon-and-rosemary). (📞93 023 24 92; www.facebook.com/espaijoliu; Carrer Badajoz 95; ⏱9am-7pm Mon-Fri, 10am-3pm Sat; 📶; Ⓜ Llacuna)

Bodega Vidrios y Cristales

WINE BAR

19 Ⓖ MAP P96, B6

In a history-steeped, stone-floored 1840 building, this atmospheric little jewel recreates an old-style neighbourhood bodega with tins of sardines, anchovies and other delicacies lining the shelves (and used in exquisite tapas, €3 to €15), house-made vermouth and a wonderful array of wines, including Andalucian *manzanilla* (sherry from Sanlúcar de Barrameda). A handful of upturned wine barrels let you rest your glass. (🖉93 250 45 01; www.gruposagardi.com; Passeig d'Isabel II 6; ⏰noon-midnight; Ⓜ Barceloneta)

Balius COCKTAIL BAR

20 Ⓠ MAP P96, E1

There's an old-fashioned jauntiness to this vintage-style cocktail den in El Poblenou, marked by its original-period exterior with tiles and gin bottles in the window. Staff pour classic cocktails (€8 to €10) as well as vermouths, and there's a small tapas menu (€3 to €7) of nachos, cheeses, *patates braves* and so on. Stop by on Sunday for live jazz around 8pm. (🖉93 315 86 50; www.baliusbar.com; Carrer de Pujades 196; ⏰5.30pm-1.30am Mon-Wed, to 2.30am Thu, 5pm-3am Fri & Sat, 5pm-1.30am Sun; Ⓜ Poblenou)

Madame George COCKTAIL BAR

21 Ⓠ MAP P96, E1

A theatrical elegance marks the interior of this small, chandelier-lit lounge just off the Rambla del Poblenou. Deft bartenders stir well-balanced cocktails like a Lychee-tini (€9; vanilla-infused vodka, fresh lychees, homemade

lychee liqueur and lime juice) in vintage glassware, while a DJ spins vinyl (mainly soul and funk) in the corner. (www.madamegeorgebar.com; Carrer de Pujades 179; ⏰6pm-2am Mon-Thu, to 3am Fri & Sat, to 12.30am Sun; Ⓜ Poblenou)

BlackLab MICROBREWERY

22 Ⓠ MAP P96, B6

Barcelona's first brewhouse opened in 2014 inside the 19th-century Palau de Mar (p98). Its taps feature 16 house-made brews, including saisons, double IPAs and dry stouts, and brewmaster Matt Boder is constantly experimenting. The kitchen sizzles up Asian-American bites (€4 to €10): burgers, dumplings, ramen. One-hour tours (€20; English/Spanish 5pm/6pm Sunday) take you behind the scenes, with a four-beer tasting. (🖉93 221 83 60; www.blacklab.es; Plaça de Pau Vila 1; ⏰10.30am-2am daily Mar-Oct, 4-11pm Mon-Thu, 11.30am-1am Fri-Sun Nov-Feb; Ⓜ Barceloneta)

La Violeta WINE BAR

23 Ⓠ MAP P96, C7

A regularly changing line-up of natural wines (glass €3.50 to €5.50), both Spanish and international, wanders into the spotlight at this cosy bar with terrace tables and mismatched wooden furniture. There are plenty of exciting Catalan picks (try the Conca de Barberà *albariño* blend), as well as lovingly made slow-food tapas (€6 to €10) starring market-fresh fish and home-grown vegetables. (☎93 221 95 81; www.facebook.com/lavioletavinosnaturales; Carrer del Baluard 58; ⏰1-11pm; Ⓜ Barceloneta)

Entertainment

Razzmatazz
LIVE MUSIC

24 MAP P96, C2

Bands from far and wide occasionally create scenes of near-hysteria at Razzmatazz, one of the city's classic live-music and clubbing venues. Bands appear throughout the week (check online), while on weekends live music gives way to club sounds. Five different rooms, with offerings varying from night to night, in one huge postindustrial space attract people of all dance persuasions and ages. (☎93 320 82 00; www.salarazzmatazz.com; Carrer de Pamplona 88; tickets from €10; ⏰hours vary; Ⓜ Bogatell)

Shopping

Palo Market Fest
MARKET

25 MAP P96, F1

One of the city's most loved events, festival-vibe Palo Market takes over an old Poblenou warehouse wreathed in flowers and greenery once a month. Local creatives – from up-and-coming fashion and jewellery designers to organic-cosmetics sellers and vintage experts – set up stalls alongside sizzling street-food trucks and lively vermouth bars, and there are also arty workshops. (☎93 159 66 70; www.palomarketfest.com; Carrer dels Pellaires 30; adult/child €4.50/free; ⏰11am-9pm 1st Sunday of month; Ⓜ Selva de Mar)

Mercat dels Encants
MARKET

26 🔒 MAP P96, B1

In a gleaming open-sided complex near Plaça de les Glòries Catalanes, the 'Market of Charms' is Barcelona's biggest flea market, and one of Europe's oldest, with its roots in medieval times. More than 500 vendors ply their wares beneath massive mirror-like panels. It's all here, from antique furniture to secondhand clothes. There's a lot of junk, plus the odd *ganga* (bargain). (Fira de Bellcaire; ☎93 245 22 99; www.facebook.com/EncantsBarcelona; Plaça de les Glòries Catalanes; ⏰9am-8pm Mon, Wed & Sat, 10am-5pm Fri & Sun; Ⓜ Glòries)

Explore ⚙

La Sagrada Família & L'Eixample

The elegant (traffic-filled) district of L'Eixample (pro-nounced 'lay-sham-pluh') is a showcase for Barce-lona's great Modernista architecture, including Gaudí's unfinished masterpiece, La Sagrada Família, spread along broad boulevards. L'Eixample also has a cele-brated dining scene, along with high-end boutiques and wildly diverse nightlife, including the buzzing LGBTIQ+ clubs of the 'Gaixample'.

The Short List

○ **La Sagrada Família (p108)** *Seeing history being made at Spain's most-visited monument and Gaudí's greatest legacy, still under construction.*

○ **La Pedrera (p112)** *Wandering through this rippling Gaudí masterpiece and its superbly preserved early-20th-century apartment.*

○ **Casa Batlló (p114)** *Marvelling at the swirling, almost-alive facade of this Gaudí-designed home with wave-shaped window frames and balconies.*

○ **Fundació Antoni Tàpies (p120)** *Deciphering the fascinating contemporary art of leading 20th-century Catalan artist Antoni Tàpies.*

Getting There & Around

Ⓜ Three lines stop at Passeig de Gràcia. Línia 3 stops at Diagonal for La Pedrera; Línies 2 and 5 stop at Sagrada Família.

🚇 FGC lines from Plaça de Catalunya take you to Provença in L'Eixample.

Neighbourhood Map on p118

La Sagrada Familia (p108) DANCAR/SHUTTERSTOCK©

Top Experience 📷

Discover Gaudí's spectacular Sagrada Família

Gaudí's unparalleled, Unesco-listed Sagrada Família inspires awe by its sheer verticality. Still under construction, work is hoped to be completed in 2026, a century after the architect's death (though the COVID-19 pandemic has caused delays). Spain's most visited monument, with 4.5 million annual visitors, the cathedral is rich in symbolism, at once ancient and thoroughly modern.

◎ MAP P118, F1

☑ 93 208 04 14; www.sagradafamilia.org; Carrer de la Marina; adult/child €20/free; ⏱9am-8pm Apr-Sep, to 7pm Mar & Oct, to 6pm Nov-Feb; Ⓜ Sagrada Família

A Holy Mission

The Temple Expiatori de la Sagrada Família (Expiatory Temple of the Holy Family) was Antoni Gaudí's all-consuming obsession. Given the commission in 1882 by a conservative society that wished to build a temple as atonement for the city's sins of modernity, Gaudí saw its completion as his holy mission. As funds dried up, he contributed his own. In all, he spent 43 years on La Sagrada Família.

Gaudí devised a temple 95m long and 60m wide, able to seat over 13,000 people, with a central tower 170m high above the transept (representing Christ) and another 17 of 100m or more. At Gaudí's death, only the crypt, the apse walls, one portal and one tower had been finished. Work began again in 1952, but controversy has always clouded progress. Opponents of the continuation of the project claim that the computer models based on what little of Gaudí's plans survived the anarchists' ire have led to the creation of a monster that has little to do with Gaudí's plans and style.

The Interior & the Apse

The roof is held up by a forest of innovative, extraordinary angled pillars. As the pillars soar towards the ceiling, they sprout a web of supporting branches, creating the effect of a forest canopy. The pillars vary in colour and load-bearing strength, from the soft Montjuïc stone pillars along the lateral aisles through to granite, dark grey basalt and finally burgundy-tinged Iranian porphyry for the key columns at the intersection of the nave and transept. The stained glass, divided in shades of red, blue, green, yellow and ochre, creates a hypnotic, magical atmosphere when the sun hits the windows.

★ Top Tips

o Book all tickets online. Guided 50-minute tours (adult/child €27/9) run in various languages. Alternatively, book tickets with audio guides (€26/free), or a trip (by lift and stairs) inside the towers on either the Nativity or Passion facades (€33/free).

o Hats, see-through clothing, low necklines and exposed backs/midriffs/shoulders aren't permitted. Shorts and skirts must be at least mid-thigh.

o Don't miss the nearby Recinte Modernista de Sant Pau (p120).

✗ Take a Break

The immediate area is packed with tourist-oriented restaurants, but locally loved **Can Pizza** (☏ 93 436 40 43; www.canpizza.eu; Passatge de Simó 21; pizzas €9-15; ⊙1-4pm & 8-11pm; ✗; ⓂSagrada Família) is perfect for gourmet pizzas. Or wander 800m south to up-and-coming Passeig de Sant Joan (p124).

Nativity Facade

The northeastern Nativity Facade (Façana del Naixement) is the artistic pinnacle of the building, mostly created under Gaudí's personal supervision. The four towers are destined to hold tubular bells capable of playing complex music at great volume; their upper parts are decorated with mosaics spelling out 'Sanctus, Sanctus, Sanctus, Hosanna in Excelsis, Amen, Alleluia'. The portal represents from left to right, Hope, Charity and Faith, and is a forest of sculpture (Gaudí used plaster casts of local people). At the top is a green cypress tree, a refuge in a storm for the white doves of peace dotted over it.

Passion Facade & Schools of Gaudí

The southwest Passion Facade (Façana de la Passió), on the theme of Christ's last days and death, was built between 1954 and 1978 based on surviving drawings by Gaudí, with four towers and a large, sculpture-bedecked portal – but was only officially completed in 2018. The late sculptor Josep Maria Subirachs (1927–2014) worked on its decoration from 1986 to 2006. He did not attempt to imitate Gaudí, instead producing angular, controversial images of his own. The main series of sculptures, on three levels, are in an S-shaped sequence, starting with the Last Supper at the bottom left and ending with Christ's burial at the top right.

La Sagrada Família's Passion Facade

Antoni Gaudí

Antoni Gaudí i Cornet (1852–1926) was born in Reus, trained initially in metalwork and obtained his architecture degree in 1878, and was both a devout Catholic and a Catalan nationalist. Although part of the Modernisme movement, Gaudí had a style all his own. A recurring theme was his obsession with the harmony of natural forms. Straight lines are eliminated, and the lines between real and unreal, sober and dream-drunk are all blurred. The grandeur of his vision was matched by an obsession with detail, as evidenced by his use of lifelike sculpture on the Nativity Facade.

With age he became almost exclusively motivated by stark religious conviction and from 1915 he gave up all other projects to devote himself to La Sagrada Família. When he died in June 1926 (he was knocked down by a tram on Gran Via de les Corts Catalanes), less than a quarter of La Sagrada Família had been completed. In 2000, the Vatican decided to proceed with the case for canonising Gaudí.

Immediately in front of the Passion Facade, the Schools of Gaudí (Escoles de Gaudí) was constructed as a children's school in 1909, with an undulating classic-Gaudí brick roof that brings to mind La Pedrera (p112).

Glory Facade

The Glory Facade (Façana de la Glòria) will, like the others, be crowned by four towers – the total of 12 representing the Twelve Apostles. Gaudí wanted it to be the most magnificent facade of the church. Inside will be the narthex, a kind of foyer made up of 16 'lanterns', a series of hyperboloid forms topped by cones. Further decoration will make the whole building a microcosmic symbol of the Christian church, with Christ represented by a massive 170m central tower above the transept, and the five remaining towers under construction symbolising the Virgin Mary and the four evangelists.

Museu Gaudí & Crypt

Open at the same times as the church, the Museu Gaudí, below ground level next to the Passion Facade, meanders through interesting material on Gaudí's life and other works, as well a re-creation of his modest office as it was when he died, and explanations of the geometric patterns and plans at the heart of his building techniques. A side hall towards the eastern end of the museum leads to a window above the simple crypt in which the genius is buried. The neo-Gothic crypt, where Masses are now held, can only be accessed from Carrer de Sardenya; it's the oldest part of the entire structure and largely the work of Gaudí's predecessor, Francisco de Paula del Villar y Lozano.

Top Experience 📷

Check out the stunning architecture of La Pedrera

In the top tier of Gaudí's achievements, this madcap Unesco-listed masterpiece, with 33 balconies, was built in 1905–10 as a combined apartment and office block. Formally called Casa Milà, after the businessman who commissioned it, it is better known as La Pedrera (the Quarry) because of its uneven grey stone facade, which ripples around the corner of Carrer de Provença.

◎ MAP P118, D2

www.lapedrera.com

Passeig de Gràcia 92

adult/child 7-12 yr from €25/14; ⊙9am-8.30pm & 9-11pm Mar-Oct, 9am-6.30pm & 7-9pm Nov-Feb

Ⓜ Diagonal

The Facade

When commissioned to design La Pedrera, Gaudí wanted to top anything else done in L'Eixample (including adding parking space – Pere Milà was one of the city's first car owners).

The natural world was one of the most enduring influences on Gaudí's work, and the building's undulating grey-stone facade evokes a cliff-face sculpted by waves and wind. The wave effect is emphasised by elaborate wrought-iron balconies that bring to mind seaweed washed up on the shore. The lasting impression is of a building on the verge of motion – a living building.

The Roof Terrace

Gaudí's blend of mischievous form with ingenious functionality is evident on the extraordinary rooftop, with its clusters of chimneys, stairwells and ventilation towers that rise and fall atop the structure's wave-like contours like giant medieval knights. Some are unadorned, others are decorated with *trencadís* (ceramic fragments) or even broken *cava* bottles. The deep patios, which Gaudí treated like interior facades, flood the apartments with natural light.

Espai Gaudí

One floor below the roof, with 270 gracious parabolic brick arches, the attic's Espai Gaudí feels like the fossilised ribcage of some giant prehistoric beast, and hosts a modest museum.

El Pis de la Pedrera

Below the attic, the elegantly furnished apartment – Gaudí's vision of domestic bliss – is done up in the style a well-to-do family might have enjoyed in the early 20th century. The sensuous curves, rippling distribution and unexpected touches in everything from light fittings to bedsteads, from door handles to balconies, might seem admirable to us today, but not everyone thought so at the time.

★ **Top Tips**

○ Buy tickets online (saving €3 on most ticket types) for opening time to avoid the worst of the crowds.

○ 'Premium' tickets (adult/child €32/14) skip the queue.

○ La Pedrera hosts superb open-air performances on the roof in summer; check online.

✕ **Take a Break**

A 300m walk southwest of La Pedrera, **La Bodegueta Provença** (☎93 215 17 25; www.provenca. labodegueta.cat; Carrer de Provença 233; tapas €6-15, mains €10-16; ⊙7am-1.45am Mon-Fri, 8am-1.45am Sat, 1pm-12.45am Sun; 🛜; 🚇FGC Provença) is a classy spot serving first-rate tapas and wines. An excellent choice any time, **Cerveseria Catalana** (☎93 216 03 68; Carrer de Mallorca 236; tapas €4-14; ⊙8am-1.30am Mon-Fri, from 9am Sat & Sun; 🚇FGC Provença) is 400m southwest near the Rambla de Catalunya.

Top Experience 📷

Stare in wonder at Casa Batlló

One of Europe's strangest residential buildings, Casa Batlló (built 1904–06) is Gaudí at his fantastical best. From its playful facade and marine-world inspiration to its revolutionary experiments in light and architectural form (straight lines are few and far between), this apartment block is one of the most beautiful buildings in a city where the architectural stakes soar sky-high.

⊙ MAP P118, E4

📞 93 216 03 06

www.casabatllo.es

Passeig de Gràcia 43

adult/child over 6 yr
€29/26

🕒 9am-8pm, last
admission 7pm

Ⓜ Passeig de Gràcia

The Facade

To Salvador Dalí, Casa Batlló's facade resembled 'twilight clouds in water'. Others see a more-than-passing resemblance to the impressionist masterpiece *Water Lilies* by Claude Monet. It's certainly exquisite and whimsical, sprinkled with fragments of blue, mauve and green tiles, and studded with wave-shaped window frames and mask-like balconies that look like the bony jaws of some strange beast – hence the nickname *casa dels ossos* (house of bones).

Sala Principal

The internal light wells shimmer with tiles of deep-sea blue. Gaudí eschewed the straight line, and so the staircase wafts you up to the 1st (main) floor. In the main salon, the ceiling twists into a whirlpool-like vortex around its sun-like chandelier; the doors, windows and skylights are dreamy waves of wood and coloured glass in mollusc-like shapes. The sense of light and space here is extraordinary thanks to the wall-length window onto Passeig de Gràcia.

Back Terrace & Roof

Pass the interior courtyard (with its pale-blue cascading wave) to Casa Batlló's back terrace: a fantasy garden in miniature, opening on to an expansive L'Eixample patio. Flowerpots take on strange forms and the accumulation of more than 300 *trencadís* (broken ceramic pieces) have the effect of immersing you in a kaleidoscope.

With its twisting chimney pots so characteristic of Gaudí's structures, the roof is Casa Batlló's grand crescendo. It was built to look like the shape of an animal's back, with shiny scales – the 'spine' changes colour as you walk around. The eastern end represents Sant Jordi (St George) and the Dragon; one local name for Casa Batlló is the *casa del drac* (house of the dragon).

★ Top Tips

○ To avoid the worst of the queues, buy tickets online (which also saves a few euros) and go first thing.

○ Alternatively, an early-bird ticket (€39) gets you in at 8.30am pre-opening. It's free for kids under seven, but they'll need to book a ticket.

○ Even if you've already visited, wander past after sunset to see the facade illuminated in all its glory.

✗ Take a Break

Around 300m down the hill just off the east side of Passeig de Gràcia, Tapas 24 (p125) is one of Barcelona's most innovative tapas bars.

Or you can head 400m north to the gorgeous garden cafe at the Alma hotel (p127).

Walking Tour 🚶

Shop in the Quadrat d'Or

While visitors to L'Eixample do the sights, barce-lonins go shopping in the Quadrat d'Or (Golden Square), the grid of streets either side of Passeig de Gràcia. This is Barcelona at its most fashion- and design-conscious, which also describes a large proportion of L'Eixample's residents. All the big names are here, alongside the boutiques of local designers who capture the essence of Barcelona cool.

Walk Facts

Start Lurdes Bergada; Ⓜ Diagonal

End Dr Bloom; Ⓜ Passeig de Gràcia

Length 1.4km; three to five hours

❶ Lurdes Bergada

Run by mother-and-son designer team Lurdes Bergada and Syngman Cucala, **Lurdes Bergada** (☎93 218 48 51; www.lurdesbergada.es; Rambla de Catalunya 112; ⏱10.30am-8.30pm Mon-Sat; Ⓜ Diagonal) delivers much-anticipated classy men's and women's fashions using natural fibres.

❷ Mauri

Few bakeries have such a pedigree as **Mauri** (☎93 215 10 20; www.pasteleriasmauri.com; Rambla de Catalunya 102; pastries €3-7; ⏱8am-midnight Mon-Fri, 9am-midnight Sat, 9am-4.30pm Sun). Ever since it opened in 1929, this grand old pastry shop and teahouse has dazzled regulars with spectacular sweets, chocolate croissants and feather-light *ensaïmades* (Balearic-style sweet buns).

❸ Purificación García

Spanish designer **Purificación García's** (☎93 496 13 36; www.purificaciongarcia.com; Carrer de Provença 292; ⏱10am-8.30pm Mon-Sat) collections are breathtaking as much for their breadth as anything else, from light summer dresses to men's ties.

❹ Bagués-Masriera

In harmony with its location, inside the Modernista **Casa Amatller** (p120), the team from **Bagués-Masriera** (☎93 216 01 74; www.bagues-masriera.com; Passeig de Gràcia 41; ⏱10am-8.30pm Mon-Fri, 11am-8pm Sat) have been chipping away at precious stones and moulding metal since the 19th century.

❺ Loewe

Loewe (☎93 216 04 00; www.loewe.com; Passeig de Gràcia 35; ⏱10am-8.30pm Mon-Sat, noon-8pm Sun) is one of Spain's leading and oldest luxury fashion stores, founded in 1846. Bags and suitcases in every colour of butter-soft leather are the mainstay.

❻ Cacao Sampaka

Chocoholics will love sleek **Cacao Sampaka** (☎93 272 08 33; www.cacaosampaka.com; Carrer del Consell de Cent 292; ⏱9am-9pm Mon-Sat). Load up on every conceivable flavour or hit the cafe for a classic *xocolata* (hot chocolate).

❼ Dr Bloom

A new collection comes out every month at bright local brand **Dr Bloom** (☎93 315 41 89; www.drbloom.es; Rambla de Catalunya 30; ⏱10am-9pm Mon-Sat), which designs and makes all its own pieces in Barcelona. The label's dresses, tops, jumpers, shawls, bags and more channel bold prints and colours no matter the season.

La Sagrada Família & L'Eixample

For reviews see
- ◉ Top Experiences p108
- ◉ Sights p120
- ✖ Eating p122
- 🍷 Drinking p126
- 🔒 Shopping p128

C del Torrent de l'Olla

C de Luís Antúnez

C Gran de Gràcia

C de la Riera de Sant Miquel

C de Bonavista

C del Còrsega

Via Augusta

C de Sèneca

Pg de Gràcia

Plaça del Cinc d'Oros

● Palau Baró de Quadras

Diagonal Ⓜ

C de la Granada del Penedès

C de Balmes

C de Tuset

2

Av Diagonal

● Casa Serra

La Pedrera ◉

La Dama ●

C d'Enric Granados

C de Balmes

Diagonal Ⓜ

Pg de Gràcia

Rambla de Catalunya

27 🔒

C d'Aribau

3

C del Rosselló

7 ✖

C de Paris

17 ◉

🍷 21

13 ✖

Provença Ⓜ

C de Còrsega

C de Muntaner

L'ESQUERRA DE L'EIXAMPLE

✖16

C de Casanova

✖ 15

4

Plaça del Doctor Ferrer Cajigal

22 🍷

C de Mallorca

C d'Aragó

Museu del Modernisme Barcelona

6 ◉

Hospital Clínic Ⓜ

C de Provença

C de València

Plaça del Doctor Letamendi

5

C del Comte d'Urgell

✖ 8

C de Villarroel

C d'Enric Granados

12 ✖

20 🍷

18 🍷

C d'Aribau

C del Comte Borrell

C de Casanova

C de Muntaner

10 ✖

C del Consell de Cent

C de la Diputació

Gran Via de les Corts Catalanes

6

Av de Roma

C d'Aragó

✖ 9

E   C de Rosselló   F   Palau Macaya   G   H

Verdaguer   C de Bailén   2   La Sagrada Família

Casa de los Punxes   4   Av Diagonal   C de Roger de Flor   C de Nàpols   1

C de Provença   C de Girona   C de València   Pg de Sant Joan   Granja Petitbo   Chichalimoná

C de Roger de Llúria   C de Mallorca   C d'Aragó   Parking Pizza   2

Palau Montaner   C del Bruc   26   23

C de Pau Claris   24   C del Consell de Cent   C de Bailén   Plaça de Tetuan

Girona   C de la Diputació   Tetuan   3

LA DRETA DE L'EIXAMPLE   C de la Diputació

Passeig de Gràcia   Casa Batlló   Gran Via de les Corts Catalanes   14   C de Girona

1   Casa Amatller   C del Bruc   4

3   Casa Lleó Morera   5   11   C de Roger de Llúria   C de Casp   Casa Calvet   C d'Ausias Marc

Fundació Antoni Tàpies   C de Pau Claris   Ronda de Sant Pere

Rambla de Catalunya   Jardins de la Reina Victòria   Pg de Gràcia   Plaça d'Urquinaona   C de Trafalgar

Urquinaona   Ronda de Sant Pere   C de les Jonqueres   Palau de la Música Catalana   5

Universitat de Barcelona   25   19   Catalunya   Urquinaona   Via Laietana

Plaça de Catalunya   Av del Portal de l'Àngel

Plaça de la Universitat   C de Bergara   Catalunya   C Comtal   BARRI GÒTIC   6

Universitat   C de Pelai   La Rambla   C de Santa Anna

Ronda de Sant Antoni   C dels Tallers   N   0   200 m   0   0.1 miles

EL RAVAL   E   F   G   H

Sights

Fundació Antoni Tàpies
GALLERY

1 ⊚ MAP P118, E4

The Fundació Antoni Tàpies is both a pioneering Modernista building (completed in the early 1880s) and the major collection of leading 20th-century Catalan artist Antoni Tàpies. Tàpies died in February 2012, aged 88. Known for his esoteric work, he left behind a powerful range of paintings and a foundation intended to promote contemporary artists. (☎93 487 03 15; www.fundaciotapies.org; Carrer d'Aragó 255; adult/child €8/free; ☺10am-7pm Tue-Thu & Sat, to 9pm Fri, to 3pm Sun; Ⓜ Passeig de Gràcia)

Recinte Modernista de Sant Pau
ARCHITECTURE

2 ⊚ MAP P118, F1

Domènech i Montaner outdid himself as architect and philanthropist with the Modernista Hospital de la Santa Creu i de Sant Pau, renamed the 'Recinte Modernista' in 2014. Built between 1902 and 1930, it was long considered one of Barcelona's most important hospitals, but was repurposed into cultural centres, offices and a monument in 2009. A joint Unesco World Heritage site together with the Palau de la Música Catalana (p84), the 27-building complex is lavishly decorated and each of its 16 pavilions unique. (☎93 553 78 01; www.santpaubarcelona.org; Carrer de Sant Antoni Maria Claret 167; adult/child €15/free, audio guide €4; ☺9.30am-6.30pm Mon-Sat, to 2.30pm Sun Apr-Oct, 9.30am-4.30pm Mon-Sat, to 2.30pm Sun Nov-Mar; Ⓜ Sant Pau/Dos de Maig)

Casa Amatller
ARCHITECTURE

3 ⊚ MAP P118, E4

One of Puig i Cadafalch's most striking flights of Modernista fantasy, Casa Amatller combines Gothic window frames and Romanesque flourishes with a stepped gable borrowed from Dutch urban architecture. But the busts and reliefs of dragons, knights and other characters dripping off the main facade are pure caprice. The building was renovated in 1900 for chocolate baron and philanthropist Antoni Amatller (1851–1910). (☎93 216 01 75; www.amatller.org; Passeig de Gràcia 41; adult/child 7-12 yr 1hr guided tour €24/12, 40min multimedia tour €19/9.50; ☺10am-6pm; Ⓜ Passeig de Gràcia)

Casa de les Punxes
ARCHITECTURE

4 ⊚ MAP P118, E1

Puig i Cadafalch's 1905 Casa Terrades is known as the Casa de les Punxes (House of Spikes) because of its pointed tile-adorned turrets. Resembling a medieval castle, this former apartment block is the only fully detached building in L'Eixample, and opened to the public only in 2017. Visits (with multilanguage audio guide) take in its stained-glass bay windows, handsome iron staircase, hydraulic floors, pillars and arches with floral motifs, and rooftop. Guided midday tours run in Spanish (Saturday) and Catalan (Sunday). (Casa Terrades; 📞93 018 52 42; www.casadelespunxes.com; Avinguda Diagonal 420; adult/child €13.50/10, tour €20/16; ⊗10am-7pm; Ⓜ Diagonal)

Casa Lleó Morera   ARCHITECTURE

5 ◉ MAP P118, E4

Domènech i Montaner's 1905 contribution to the Illa de la Discòrdia, with Modernista carving outside and a bright, tiled lobby in which floral motifs predominate, is perhaps the least odd-looking of the three main buildings on the block. It's now occupied by luxury fashion store Loewe (p117). (Passeig de Gràcia 35; Ⓜ Passeig de Gràcia)

Museu del Modernisme Barcelona   MUSEUM

6 ◉ MAP P118, D5

Housed in a stuccoed, red-washed 1902 Modernista building by Enric Sagnier, this museum seems like a big Modernista-furniture showroom. Several pieces by Gaudí, including chairs from Casa Batlló and a mirror and chair from Casa Calvet, appear alongside a host of creations by his lesser-known contemporaries.

La Sagrada Família & L'Eixample Sights

Casa Batlló (p114) and Casa Amatller

Lesser-Known Modernisme

Palau Macaya (Map p118, F1; 📞 93 457 95 31; www.obrasocial lacaixa.org; Passeig de Sant Joan 108; admission free; ⏱ 9am-8pm Mon-Fri; Ⓜ Verdaguer) A little-known Modernisme gem by Josep Puig i Cadafalch.

Palau Montaner (Map p118, E2; 📞 93 317 76 52; www.funda ciotapies.org; Carrer de Mallorca 278; adult/child €7/free; ⏱ by reservation; Ⓜ Passeig de Grà-cia) A spectacular, sculpture-filled Domènech i Montaner mansion (dating from 1893); book visits through the Fundació Antoni Tàpies (re-serves@ftapies.com).

Casa Calvet (Map p118, G4; Carrer de Casp 48; Ⓜ Urquinaona, Tetuan) Gaudí's most conventional, baroque-inspired contribution (1901).

(📞 93 272 28 96; www.mmbcn.cat; Carrer de Balmes 48; adult/child €10/5; ⏱ 10.30am-2pm & 4-7pm Mon-Fri, 10.30am-2pm Sat; Ⓜ Passeig de Gràcia)

Eating

Lasarte   MODERN EUROPEAN €€€

7 ✖ MAP P118, D3

One of Barcelona's preeminent restaurants – and its first to gain three Michelin stars (in 2016) – Lasarte is overseen by lauded chef Martín Berasategui, and headed up by Paolo Casa-grande. Serving up extraordinary dishes from the likes of Duroc pig's trotters with Jerusalem artichoke to squid tartare with kaffir consommé, this is seriously sophisticated, seasonally inspired cookery. Yet it's all served in an ultra-contemporary dining room by staff who could put the most overawed diners at ease. (📞 93 445 32 42; www.restaurantlasarte. com; Carrer de Mallorca 259; mains €52-70; ⏱ 1.30-3pm & 8.30-10pm Tue-Sat; Ⓜ Diagonal)

Disfrutar   MODERN EUROPEAN €€€

8 ✖ MAP P118, A5

Holding two-Michelin-stars, Disfrutar ('Enjoy') is among the city's finest restaurants. Run by alumni of Ferran Adrià's game-changing El Bulli, nothing is as it seems, such as black and green olives that are actually chocolate ganache with orange-blossom water. The Mediterranean-inspired decor is fabulously on point, with latticed brickwork and trademark geo-metric ceramics from Catalan design team Equipo Creativo, and service is faultless. (📞 93 348 68 96; www.disfrutarbar celona.com; Carrer de Villarroel 163; tasting menus €155-195; ⏱ 1-2.15pm & 8-9.15pm Mon-Fri; 🖋; Ⓜ Hospital Clínic)

Modernisme

Barcelona's flamboyant Modernisme buildings emerged during the late 19th century, a period of great artistic and political fervour deeply connected to Catalan identity, and which transformed early-20th-century Barcelona into a showcase for avant-garde architecture. Aiming to establish a new Catalan archetype, Antoni Gaudí and other visionary architects drew inspiration from the past, using elements from the Spanish vernacular – shapes, details and brickwork reminiscent of Islamic, Gothic and Renaissance designs.

Gaudí

Leading the Modernista way was Antoni Gaudí i Cornet (1852–1926), who was a Catalan nationalist. Gaudí took great inspiration from Gothic styles, but he also sought to emulate the harmony he observed in nature. The architect's work is an earthy appeal to sinewy movement, yet often with a dreamlike or surreal quality, eliminating straight lines and blurring boundaries. **Casa Batlló** (p114) and **La Pedrera** (p112) are fine examples in which all appears a riot of the unnaturally natural – or the naturally unnatural. But Gaudí's masterpiece was **La Sagrada Família** (p108), which he took over in 1883; in it you can see the culminating vision of many ideas developed over the years.

Other Architects

Lluís Domènech i Montaner (1850–1923) and Josep Puig i Cadafalch (1867–1956) left a wealth of remarkable buildings across Barcelona, while the Rome-trained sculptor Eusebi Arnau (1863–1933) was one of the most popular figures called upon to decorate Barcelona's Modernista piles, including the **Hospital de la Santa Creu i de Sant Pau** (p120), the **Palau de la Música Catalana** (p84) and **Casa Amatller** (p120).

Materials & Decorations

Modernista architects relied on artisan skills that have now been all but relegated to history. Stone, unclad brick, exposed iron and steel frames, and the copious use of stained glass and ceramics in decoration, were all features of the new style. The craftspeople required for these tasks were the heirs of the guild masters and had absorbed centuries of know-how, which was also applied to newly arrived forged iron and steel. Gaudí even ran schools at La Sagrada Família's workshops to keep these old skills alive.

Passeig de Sant Joan

Head over to ever-trendier boulevard Passeig de Sant Joan, in eastern L'Eixample, for a fashionable local drinking-and-dining scene.

Parking Pizza (Map p118, H2; 📞 93 541 80 11; www.parkingpizza.com; Passeig de Sant Joan 56; mains €11-15; ⏱1-4pm & 8-11pm Sun-Fri, to midnight Sat; 🖋 ; Ⓜ Tetuan) Sprawling warehouse cooking up outrageously popular wood-fired pizzas and perfect stuffed pita.

Granja Petitbo (Map p118, G1; 📞 93 265 65 03; www.granjapetitbo.com; Passeig de Sant Joan 82; mains €5-11; ⏱8.30am-11.30pm Mon-Fri, 10am-midnight Sat, 10am-11.30pm Sun; 🛜 🖋 ; Ⓜ Girona) This sunny corner cafe has an all-day local-produce menu and terrific coffee.

Chichalimoná (Map p118, G2; 📞 93 277 64 03; www.chichalimona.com; Passeig de Sant Joan 80; mains €12-17; ⏱9.30am-1am Tue-Thu, to 2am Fri & Sat, to 5pm Sun; 🛜 ; Ⓜ Girona) Loved for its global-inspired plates, weekend brunches and vermouth-hour bites.

Cinc Sentits

CATALAN €€€

9 🍴 MAP P118, C6

Enter the realm of the 'Five Senses' to indulge in jaw-dropping eight- or 11-course tasting menus of small, experimental dishes concocted by chef Jordi Artal (there's no à la carte available, although dishes can be tweaked on request for dietary requirements). The use of fresh local produce, such as Costa Brava line-caught fish and top-quality Extremadura suckling pig, is key at this elegant Michelin-star address. (📞 93 323 94 90; www.cincsentits.com; Carrer d'Entença 60; tasting menus €99-119; ⏱1.30-2.30pm & 8.30-9.30pm Tue-Sat; 🖋 ; Ⓜ Rocafort)

Mont Bar

BISTRO €€€

10 🍴 MAP P118, D6

Named for the owner's Val d'Aran hometown, this stylish space with black-and-white floors, pine-green booths and bottle-lined walls offers next-level cooking fired by organic, seasonal ingredients, many of them home-grown. Exquisite tapas (such as corn-and-jalapeño crisp-bread and oyster with mandarin tiger's milk) precede superb small-plate mains, such as celery risotto with truffle, and show-stopping desserts. Stunning wines (more than 250) span all price points. Reservations recommended. (📞 93 323 95 90; www.montbar.com; Carrer de la Diputació 220; tapas €4-10, mains €15-

30; ⏱1-4pm & 7-11.30pm Wed-Mon; 📶♿; Ⓜ Universitat)

Tapas 24   TAPAS €

11 🍴 MAP P118, F4

Hotshot chef Carles Abellán runs this basement tapas haven known for its gourmet renditions of old faves, including the *bikini* (toasted ham-and-cheese sandwich, here with truffle and cured ham), freshly cooked tortilla and zesty lemon-infused *boquerones* (anchovies). You can't book, but it's worth the wait. For dessert, try the creamy *payoyo* cheese. Before 1pm, pop in for superb *entrepans* (filled rolls) and omelettes. (📞93 488 09 77; www.carlesabellan.com; Carrer de la Diputació 269; tapas €4-12; ⏱9am-midnight; 📶; Ⓜ Passeig de Gràcia)

Pepa   TAPAS €€

12 🍴 MAP P118, C5

An old bookshop graced by original check-tiled floors and exposed-brick walls is the setting for this outstanding venture from the team behind El Born's beloved Bar del Pla (p81). Don't miss the mushroom carpaccio with straw-berries and wasabi vinaigrette, or, in season, the fabulous eggs with truffle and chips. Desserts – like flambeed berries – are just as exquisite, while wines are natural, organic and/or biodynamic. (📞93 611 18 85; www.pepapla.cat; Carrer d'Aribau 41; sharing plates €7-18; ⏱5-11pm Sun-Thu, 1-11.30pm Fri & Sat, closed 2 weeks Aug; ♿; Ⓜ Universitat)

Auto Rosellon   INTERNATIONAL €€

13 🍴 MAP P118, B3

With cornflower-blue paintwork and fresh produce on display, Auto Rosellon works mostly organic ingredients sourced from small producers and its own garden into creative dishes such as avocado toast with feta, cauliflower doused in kale pesto, *gnudi* pasta with baked pumpkin, and slow-roasted pork tacos. Homemade juices, lemonade and cakes are excep-tional, and there are natural wines, cocktails and craft beers. (📞93 853 93 20; www.autorosellon.com; Carrer del Rosselló 182; breakfasts €4-9, mains €10-15; ⏱8am-1am Mon-Wed, to 2am Thu & Fri, 9am-2am Sat, 9am-midnight Sun; 📶♿; Ⓜ Diagonal, 🚉 FGC Provença)

Spanish buffet

Hawker 45

ASIAN €€

14 MAP P118, H4

Taking its cues from an Asian hawkers market, chef Laila Bazahm's aromatic restaurant sizzles up Asian–Latin American street-food dishes such as spicy Malaysian squid laksa, Indonesian lamb satay, Indian tandoori carrots and Thai green veg curry with avocado. Dine at the long, red bar overlooking the open kitchen or in the postindustrial dining space with bare beams and wall murals. (☏93 763 83 15; www.hawker45.com; Carrer de Casp 45; mains €10-16; ☉1-4pm & 8-11pm Mon-Sat; ☝; Ⓜ Tetuan)

Gresca Bar

CATALAN €€

15 MAP P118, C4

From the team behind smart restaurant Gresca (with whom it shares an open-plan kitchen), this

La Dama

🍽

Diagonal's 1917 Modernista Casa Sayrach has been reborn as graceful gastro space **La Dama** (Map p118, A3; ☏93 209 63 28; www.la-dama.com; Avinguda Diagonal 423-425; mains €22-30; Ⓜ Diagonal, Ⓡ FGC Provença), filled with grand-yet-homey lounges, mirrors and velvet. Perfectly executed dishes wander around northern Spain, France and Italy: pork ribs with vegetable cream, squid-ink carbonara, sole meunière for two.

elegant gold-and-green wine and tapas bar is a whispered-about local hit. Chef Rafa Peña specialises in thoughtful, ambitious reinterpretations of quality seasonal produce, combined with exclusively natural wines. Try leeks sprinkled with burrata, veal sweetbreads or a *bikini* with mushrooms or pork loin and Comté cheese. (☏93 451 6193; Carrer de Provença 230; sharing plates €7-16; ☉1.30-4pm & 8.30-10.30pm; ☝; Ⓡ FGC Provença)

La Cuina d'en Garriga

SPANISH €€

16 MAP P118, C4

Tomatoes dangle above the open kitchen at this cheerful bistro-style spot with bright-red trim and checkered marble floors, popular with lunching *barcelonins*. Seasonal, organic farm-to-table menus highlight small, mostly local producers in creatively plated dishes. (☏93 250 37 00; www.lacuinadengarriga.com; Carrer d'Enric Granados 58; mains €9-20; ☉1-11pm Wed-Sun; 🛜☝; Ⓡ GFC Provença)

Drinking

Dry Martini

BAR

17 MAP P118, B3

Waiters make expert cocktail suggestions, but the house drink, taken at the gleaming wooden bar or on one of the plush green banquettes, is always a good bet – an expertly mixed martini (more than

a million are thought to have been served here). (📞93 217 50 72; www.drymartiniorg.com; Carrer d'Aribau 162-166; ⏰1pm-2.30am Mon-Thu, to 3am Fri, 6.30pm-3am Sat, 6.30pm-2.30am Sun; 🚇FGC Provença)

Cosmo   CAFE

18 🚇 MAP P118, D5

Set on a pedestrian strip just behind the university, this cool cafe/cultural space has bicycles hanging from high, white walls and bright splashy murals, and even makes a feature of its fire hose. Along with fresh juices, hot chocolate, teas and pastries, it serves arty brunches and **Nømad** (www.nomadcoffee.es; Carrer de Pujades 95; ⏰9am-5pm Mon-Fri; 🚇Bogatell) coffee, not to mention beer and wine.

All ingredients are sourced within 100km. (📞93 105 79 92; www.galeriacosmo.com; Carrer d'Enric Granados 3; ⏰10am-10pm; 🚇Universitat)

Milano   COCKTAIL BAR

19 🚇 MAP P118, F5

Subtly signed from street level, this gem of hidden Barcelona nightlife is a subterranean old-school cocktail bar with red-velvet banquettes and glass-fronted cabinets, presided over by white-jacketed waiters. Live music (Cuban, jazz, blues, flamenco, swing) plays nightly (schedules online); DJs take over after 11pm. Fantastic cocktails include the rum-infused Hemingway and seven different Bloody Marys (€10 to €15). (📞93 112 71 50; www.camparimilano.com; Ronda de la

Universitat 35; 1pm-4am, hours can vary; MCatalunya)

Garage Beer Co
CRAFT BEER

20 MAP P118, C5

One of the original craft-beer bars to pop up in Barcelona, Garage brews its own in a space at the bar and at its out-of-town brewery, and offers around 10 different styles at a time. The Ocata (a delicate session IPA) and Soup (a more robust IPA) are always on the board; other favourites include Circus Tears (an Imperial stout). (93 528 59 89; www.garagebeer.co; Carrer del Consell de Cent 261; noon-midnight Sun-Thu, to 3am Fri & Sat; MUniversitat)

Alfresco Bars

Many Barcelona hotels house wonderful open-air bars.

○ Alaire, Condes de Barcelona, L'Eixample

○ Jardí del Alma, Alma, L'Eixample

○ Batuar Terrace, Cotton House, L'Eixample

○ Jardí Diana, El Palace, L'Eixample

○ Terraza del Pulitzer, Hotel Pulitzer, L'Eixample

○ The Roof, Barcelona Edition, La Ribera

○ La Isabela, Hotel 1898, La Rambla

Monkey Factory
COCKTAIL BAR

21 MAP P118, B3

DJs spin on weekends at this high-spirited venue but it's hopping from early most nights, often hosting language-exchange sessions. Funky Monkey (triple sec, gin, lime and egg white), Chimpa Sour (cardamom-infused pisco sour) and Chita Tai (rum, lime, cacao, triple sec and almond syrup) are among the inventive cocktails mixed behind the green-neon-lit bar. (93 270 31 16; www.facebook.com/monkeyfactorybcn; Carrer de Còrsega 234; 6.30pm-3am Tue-Sat; FGC Provença)

Hemingway
COCKTAIL BAR

22 MAP P118, B4

There's often a queue out the door for a table at this intimate, speakeasy-style basement cocktail den with a tiny front terrace. International whiskies, rare gins and lightly imaginative cocktails crafted with fresh-pressed citrus juices are owner-barista Luca Izzo's specialities; try the best-selling gin-based Montgomery (infused with ginger and Earl Grey tea; €12) or a classic G&T (€12). (93 129 67 93; www.hemingwaybcn.com; Carrer de Muntaner 114; 4pm-2.30am Sun-Thu, to 3am Fri & Sat; MHospital Clínic)

Shopping

Flores Navarro
FLOWERS

23 MAP P118, F2

You never know when you might need flowers, and this vast,

packed-to-the-rafters florist never closes. Established in 1960, it has two spaces on Carrer de València, and is worth a visit just for the bank of colour and wonderful fragrance, from sky-blue roses to tiny cacti. (📞93 457 40 99; www.florist eriasnavarro.com; Carrer de València 320; ⏱24hr; Ⓜ Girona)

Joan Múrria
FOOD & DRINKS

24 📍 MAP P118, E3

Ramon Casas designed the 1898 Modernista shopfront advertisements at this temple of speciality foods from around Catalonia and beyond. Artisan cheeses, Iberian hams, caviar, canned delicacies, olive oils, smoked fish, *cavas* and wines, coffee and loose-leaf teas are among the treats in store. (Queviures Múrria; 📞93 215 57 89; www.murria.cat; Carrer de Roger de Llúria 85; ⏱10am-2pm & 5-8pm Tue-Sat; Ⓜ Girona)

Altaïr
BOOKS

25 📍 MAP P118, E5

Enter a travel wonderland at this extensive bookshop, founded in 1979, which has enough guidebooks, maps, travel literature and other works to induce a severe case of itchy feet. There's also a helpful travellers' noticeboard and cosy downstairs cafe. (📞93 342 71 71; www.altair.es; Gran Via de les Corts Catalanes 616; ⏱10am-8.30pm Mon-Sat; 🛜; Ⓜ Catalunya)

The Gaixample

The area just north of Gran Via de les Corts Catalanes and to the west of Rambla de Catalunya, popularly known as the 'Gaixample', is the heart of Barcelona's LGBTIQ+ scene, with bars, clubs and restaurants. See p27 for more information.

Mercat de la Concepció
MARKET

26 📍 MAP P118, F2

Dating from 1888 (though remodelled in 1998), the iron-clad Mercat de la Concepció has around 50 stalls selling food, flowers, wine and more, including three on-site bars. (📞93 476 48 70; www.lacon cepcio.cat; Carrer d'Aragó 313-317; ⏱8am-8pm Tue-Fri, to 3pm Mon & Sat early Sep–mid-Jul, 8am-3pm Mon-Sat mid-Jul–early Sep; Ⓜ Girona)

Avant
FASHION & ACCESSORIES

27 📍 MAP P118, B3

Taking inspiration from the world of dance and cultures around the globe, *barcelonin* designer Silvia Garcia Presas creates her elegant women's dresses, shirts, shoes and other pieces working directly with local producers. (📞93 300 76 73; www.theavant.com; Carrer d'Enric Granados 106; ⏱10.30am-8.30pm Mon-Fri, to 2.30pm Sat; Ⓜ Diagonal, ⓇFGC Provença)

Explore ⊛

Gràcia &
Park Güell

*Gràcia was an independent town until the 1890s, and
its narrow lanes and picturesque plazas still have a
village-like feel. Well-worn cafes and bars, vintage
shops and a smattering of multicultural restaurants
make it a magnet for a young, largely international
crowd. To its north lies Gaudí's outdoor Modernista
storybook of Park Güell. Recently opened Casa Vicens
is another Gaudí highlight.*

The Short List

○ **Park Güell (p132)** *Meandering along winding paths
amid the wild sculptures, mosaics and columns of
Gaudí's open-air wonderland, high above the city.*

○ **Casa Vicens (p137)** *Admiring the curious interplay
of brick, chequerboard patterns and Moorish elements
on this Unesco-listed Gaudí castle-mansion.*

○ **Mercat de la Llibertat (p137)** *Shopping for delectable local specialities (and sampling them too) at the
neighbourhood's emblematic market.*

○ **Bunkers del Carmel (p138)** *Escaping up to this
hilltop for fabulous 360-degree city panoramas.*

○ **Tapas & Squares (p139)** *Wandering between Gràcia's many charming squares and dipping into locally
loved tapas spots such as Bar Bodega Quimet.*

Getting There & Around

Ⓜ Línia 3 to Fontana and Línia 4 to Joanic are best.

🚶 Strolling northwest along Passeig de Gràcia from Plaça
de Catalunya is a lovely way to reach the neighbourhood
(1.5km walk, 25 minutes).

Neighbourhood Map on p136

Mosaic bench in Park Güell (p132) DOBLE D/GETTY IMAGES ©

Top Experience 📷

Explore enchanting Park Güell

Park Güell – around 1km north of Gràcia – is where Gaudí turned his hand and imagination to land-scape gardening. It's a surreal, enchanting place where the Modernista's passion for natural forms really took flight, to the point where the artificial almost seems more natural than the natural. Park Güell originated in 1900, when Eusebi Güell hired Gaudí to create a miniature city for the wealthy (though the project was abandoned in 1914).

◎ MAP P136, A1

📞 93 409 18 31

www.parkguell.barcelona

Carrer d'Olot 7

adult/child €10/7

🚍 H6, D40, V19, Bus Güell,
Ⓜ Lesseps, Vallcarca,
Alfons X

Plaça de la Natura, Banc de Trencadís & Sala Hipóstila

Arriving via the park's main eastern entrance, you'll reach a broad open space, the **Plaça de la Natura**, which doubles as a rainwater catchment area and whose centrepiece is the **Banc de Trencadís**, completed in 1914. Curving sinuously around the perimeter, this multicoloured tiled bench was designed by one of Gaudí's closest colleagues, architect Josep Maria Jujol (1879–1949). To the west of the square extends the **Pòrtic de la Bugadera** (the Laundry Room Portico), a gallery where the twisted stonework columns and roof give the effect of a cloister beneath tree roots – a recurring motif.

Beneath the square, opposite two immediately recognisable Hansel-and-Gretel houses and the typically curvaceous Casa del Guarda, steps lead to the **Sala Hipóstila** (the Doric Temple; pictured). This forest of 86 stone columns – some leaning like mighty trees bent by the weight of time – was originally intended as a market, with its tiled ceilings and Catalan vaults.

Casa-Museu Gaudí

Near the park's eastern entrance lies the spired dusty-pink **Casa-Museu Gaudí** (📞93 208 04 14; www.sagradafamilia.org; Carretera del Carmel 23a; adult/child €5.50/free; ⏰9am-8pm Apr-Sep, 10am-6pm Oct-Mar; 🚌V19, H6, D40, Bus Güell, 🅼Lesseps, Alfons X, Vallcarca), where Gaudí lived for almost the last 20 years of his life (1906–26). The house was built in 1904 by Francesc Berenguer i Mestres, and is now filled with Gaudí-designed furniture and ironwork.

Tours

One-hour guided tours cost €12 (plus park admission); pre-book online. Private guided tours cost €45 per person (plus admission) and require at least two people.

★ Top Tips

○ The parks' opening hours vary through the year reflecting the changing daylight hours. It's open 8am to 9.30pm May to August, to 8.30pm in April, September and October, to 6.15pm November to mid-February, and til 7pm from mid-February to March.

○ Go first thing in the morning or late in the day to beat the worst of the crowds.

○ You can visit the northern part of the park (without the Gaudí features) free of charge.

○ Prebook tickets to ensure admission and take advantage of the Bus Güell shuttle from Alfons X metro stop.

✕ Take a Break

Before or after making the trip up to the park, stop off at La Panxa del Bisbe (p139) in upper Gràcia for deliciously creative tapas and good wines.

Walking Tour 🥾

Gràcia's Village Squares

Located halfway between L'Eixample and Park Güell, Gràcia was a separate village until 1897, and its tight, narrow lanes and endless interlocking squares maintain a unique, almost village-like feel to this day. In places bohemian, in others rapidly gentrifying, Gràcia is Barcelona at its most eclectic, its nooks and crannies home to everything from soulful old taverns to eco-minded boutiques.

Walk Facts

Start Casa Fuster;
Ⓜ Diagonal

End Plaça de la Virreina;
Ⓜ Fontana, Joanic

Length 2km; 50 minutes

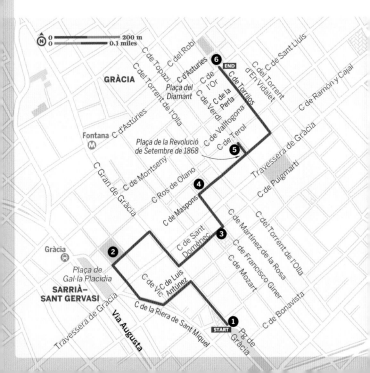

❶ Casa Fuster

Head through Passeig de Gràcia and up Carrer Gran de Gràcia into Gràcia proper, where you'll find a grand Modernista edifice now turned sumptuous hotel, **Casa Fuster** (Passeig de Gràcia 132; Ⓜ Diagonal), designed by Domènech i Montaner from 1908 to 1911.

❷ Plaça & Mercat de la Llibertat

Plaça de la Llibertat (🚇FGC Gràcia) is home to the bustling Modernista produce **market** (p137) of the same name, along with a couple of great little restaurants. The market was designed by Gaudí's protégé, Francesc Berenguer, who was busy in this part of town despite never having been awarded a diploma as an architect.

❸ Plaça de la Vila de Gràcia

Meandering east, you'll find the popular **Plaça de la Vila de Gràcia** (Ⓜ Fontana, Diagonal, 🚇FGC Gràcia), which was until 2009 named after the mayor under whom Gràcia was absorbed by Barcelona, Francesc Rius i Taulet. It's fronted by the local **town hall** (🕿 93 402 70 00; www.bcn.cat; Plaça de Sant Jaume; ⊘10am-2pm Sun), designed by Berenguer, and at its heart stands the 1862 Torre del Rellotge (Clock Tower), long a symbol of Republican agitation.

❹ Plaça del Sol

Just north lies the rowdiest of Gràcia's squares, **Plaça del Sol** (Ⓜ Fontana), where bars and restaurants come to life on long summer nights. The square was the scene of summary executions after an uprising in 1870, and, during the civil war, an air-raid shelter was installed.

❺ Plaça de la Revolució de Setembre de 1868

Nearby, this busy, elongated **square** (Ⓜ Fontana, Joanic) commemorates the toppling of Queen Isabel II, a cause of much celebration in this working-class stronghold. Long-running **Bar Canigó** (🕿 93 213 30 49; www.barcanigo.com; Carrer de Verdi 2; ⊘10am-2am Mon-Fri, from 8pm Sat; Ⓜ Fontana) here is an animated spot for house vermouth or coffee, now overseen by the third generation of owners.

❻ Plaça de la Virreina

Pleasant terraces adorn the leafy, pedestrianised **Plaça de la Virreina**, presided over by the 19th-century **Església de Sant Joan** (🕿 93 237 73 58; Plaça de la Virreina; ⊘8am-12.45pm & 4-8pm, hours can vary; Ⓜ Fontana, Joanic). The church was designed by Francesc Berenguer i Mestres, Gaudí's protégé, but it's believed that the interior chapel is the work of Gaudí himself (the jury is still out, however).

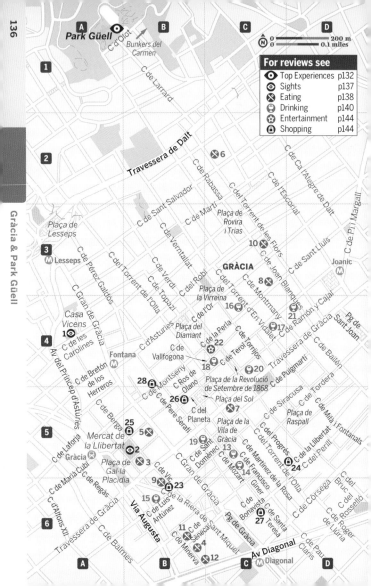

Park Güell A

C d'Olot A

Bunkers del Carmen B

C de Larrard

C de Larrard 1

For reviews see

◉	Top Experiences	p132
◉	Sights	p137
✖	Eating	p138
☕	Drinking	p140
✪	Entertainment	p144
🛍	Shopping	p144

Travessera de Dalt 2

✖ 6

C de Rabassa

C de Sant Salvador

C de Martí

C del Torrent de les Flors

C de Ca l'Alegre de Dalt

C de l'Escorial

Plaça de Lesseps

Plaça de Rovira i Trias

C de Ca l'Alegre de Dalt

C de Pi i Margall

C de Sant Lluís

10 ✖

Ⓜ Lesseps 3

C del Torrent de l'Olla

C de Verntallat

C de Verdi

C del Robí

GRÀCIA

C de Joan Blanques

8 ✖

Joanic Ⓜ

C de Pérez Galdós

C Gran de Gràcia

C de Topazi

C del Torrent d'En Vidalet

C de Montmany

21 ☕

17 ☕

Pg de Sant Joan

Casa Vicens 1 ◉ 4

C de les Carolines

Plaça de la Virreina

16 ☕

C de Ramón y Cajal

C d'Astúries

Plaça del Diamant

C del Or

C de la Perla

C de Torrijos

Travessera de Gràcia

C de Bailèn

Fontana Ⓜ

22 ✖

C de Terol

C de Puigmartí

C de Bretón de los Herreros

C de Vallfogona

18 ☕

20 ☕

C de Siracusa

28 🛍

C de Montseny

C Ros de Olano

Plaça de la Revolució de Setembre de 1868

Plaça de Raspall

C de Mília i Fontanals

C de Tordera

C del Princep d'Astúries 5

26 🛍

C del Planeta

Plaça del Sol

✖ 7

C del Progrés

C de la Llibertat

C del Perill

25 🛍

C de Berga

5 ✖

Mercat de la Llibertat ◉ 2

19 ☕

Plaça de la Vila de Gràcia

13 ☕

C de Sant Domènec

C de Martínez de la Rosa

C del Torrent de l'Olla

24 🛍

C de Còrsega

C de Bruc

C de Latòria

Gràcia 🚈

Plaça de Gal·la Placídia

☕ 3

C de Vic

9 ☕

23 🛍

14 ☕

C de Mozart

C de Francisco Giner

C de Bonavista

C de Santa Teresa

27 🛍

C del Roser de Llúria

C de Maria Cubí

C de Regàs

15 ☕

Antúnez

C de Luis Antúnez

C de la Riera de Sant Miquel

Pg de Gràcia

C de Rosselló

C d'Alfons XII

Travessera de Gràcia

C de Balmes

Via Augusta

11 ☕

C de Sant Miquel

4 ✖

C de Senècaet

C de Minerva

12 ✖

Av Diagonal

Diagonal Ⓜ

0 —— 200 m
0 —— 0.1 miles D

Sights

Casa Vicens ARCHITECTURE

1 ⊙ MAP P136, A4

A Unesco-listed masterpiece, this angular, turreted 1885-completed private house was Gaudí's inaugural commission, when the architect was aged just 30, created for stock and currency broker Manuel Vicens i Montaner. Tucked away west of Gràcia's main drag, its richly detailed facade is awash with ceramic colour and shape, including distinctive marigold tiling. It opened to the public in 2017. You're free to wander through but one-hour guided tours (in Catalan, Spanish, English and French) bring the building to life. (☏93 547 59 80; www. casavicens.org; Carrer de les Carolines 20-26; adult/child €16/12, guided tour per person additional €4; ⏰10am-8pm Apr-Sep, to 3pm Mon, to 7pm Tue-Sun Oct-Mar, last admission 1hr 20min before closing; Ⓜ Fontana)

Mercat de la Llibertat MARKET

2 ⊙ MAP P136, B5

Opened in 1888, the 'Market of Liberty' was covered in 1893 by Francesc Berenguer i Mestres (1866–1914), Gaudí's long-time assistant, in typically fizzy Modernista style, employing generous whirls of wrought iron. Despite a considerable facelift in 2009, it remains emblematic of Gràcia: full of life and fabulous fresh produce, and with places such as **El Tast de Joan Noi** (☏635 706429; www.face book.com/eltastdejoannoi; tapas €4-15;

Casa Vicens

MARCO FINE/SHUTTERSTOCK ©

Bunkers del Carmel

For magnificent 360-degree Barcelona views, head to the El Carmel neighbourhood (under a kilometre east of Park Güell) and up the Turó de la Rovira hill to the **Bunkers del Carmel viewpoint** (Turó de la Rovira; ☏93 256 21 22; https://ajuntament.barcelona.cat; Carrer de Marià Labèrnia; admission free; ☺museum 10am-2pm Wed, to 3pm Sat & Sun; ☐V19, 22, 24). Above the weeds and dusty hillside, you'll find old concrete firing platforms where students and visitors gather, especially at sunset. The platforms were part of an anti-aircraft battery during the Spanish Civil War; postwar, it was a shanty town until the early 1990s, and has lain abandoned since then. Welcoming **Las Delicias** (☏93 429 22 02; www.barrestaurantedelicias.com; Carrer de Mühlberg 1; tapas €5-13, mains €9-15; ☺10am-4pm & 7-10.30pm Tue-Thu, 10am-4pm & 8-11pm Fri & Sat; ☐24) is a great little nearby spot for tapas.

☺9am-5pm Tue-Fri, to 3pm Sat, closed Aug) offering tapas. (☏93 217 09 95; www.facebook.com/elmercatdel allibertat; Plaça de la Llibertat 27; ☺8.30am-8pm Mon-Fri, to 3pm Sat; ⓂFontana, ⓇFGC Gràcia)

Eating

La Pubilla CATALAN €€

3 🍽 MAP P136, B5

Hidden away behind a peachy-pink door by the Mercat de la Llibertat, La Pubilla specialises in hearty *'esmorzars de forquilla'* ('fork breakfasts') beloved by market workers and local residents. There's also an outrageously popular daily three-course *menú* (€16), which stars seasonal produce and Catalan dishes such as baked cod, or roast pork cheek with chickpeas; book ahead or arrive early. (☏93 218 29 94; www.

lapubilla.cat; Plaça de la Llibertat 23; mains €10-18; ☺8.30am-5pm Mon, to 11.30pm Tue-Sat; ⓂFontana)

Berbena MEDITERRANEAN €€

4 🍽 MAP P136, B6

Tucked away off busy Diagonal, Berbena specialises in ambitiously prepared, beautifully presented seasonal dishes from the open-plan kitchen. The daily-changing *menú* starts with home-baked bread, accompanied by a main such as zestily dressed burrata with pumpkin and sides of tortilla or chilled green-vegetable soup. It's a tiny, minimalist-modern space, with seats in the window and coffee from neighbouring roaster SlowMov (p141). (☏93 801 59 87; www.berbenabcn.com; Carrer de Minerva 6; set 4-dish menú €16.50; ☺7.30-11pm Mon & Sat, 1-3.30pm & 7.30-11pm Tue-Fri; ☑; ⓂDiagonal)

Botafumeiro SEAFOOD €€€

5 MAP P136, B5

A wonderful world of Galician sea-food, Botafumeiro has long been a magnet for VIPs visiting Barcelona. It's a good place to try *percebes* (goose barnacles), often considered the ultimate fruit-of-the-sea deli-cacy. You can bring the price down by sharing a marine *mitges racions* (large tapas plates), followed by mains such as baked spider crab, shellfish paella or charcoal-grilled wild hake. (📞93 218 42 30, Whatsapp 662 669337; www.botafumeiro.es; Carrer Gran de Gràcia 81; mains €22-55; 🕐noon-1am; Ⓜ Fontana)

La Panxa del Bisbe TAPAS €€

6 MAP P136, C2

With its local buzz and artfully minimalist interior, the 'Bishop's Belly' is a pleasant surprise in upper Gràcia, delivering creative tapas that earn high praise from both *barcelonins* and visitors. Feast on provolone-stuffed courgette flowers, grilled octopus with capers and celery, or Iberian ham with melon and mint. The wine list includes excellent picks from Cata-lonia and elsewhere in Spain. (📞93 313 70 49; Carrer del Torrent de les Flors 158; tapas €9-14, tasting menus €30-38; 🕐1.30-3.30pm & 8.30pm-midnight Tue-Sat; 📶📷; Ⓜ Joanic)

Extra Bar TAPAS €€

7 MAP P136, C5

At this lively pint-sized tapas bar, the team behind Gràcia's much-loved La Pubilla serves simple yet highly memorable local-rooted *pla-tillos* (sharing plates) alongside a carefully curated selection of Span-ish wines by the glass. Seasonal flavours and fresh local ingredients fuel weekly changing menus with a few Asian influences, which might feature lime-laced squid tacos, ter-rific croquettes or made-to-order omelettes. (📞93 218 29 94; www.lapubilla.cat; Carrer Torrent de l'Olla 79; raciones €5-13; 🕐6.30pm-midnight Tue-Thu, to 1am Fri, noon-3.30pm & 7.30pm-1am Sat; Ⓜ)

Les Tres a la Cuina MEDITERRANEAN €

8 MAP P136, C3

Fresh local ingredients are thrown into creative, health-focused, home-cooked mixes at this eco-aware deli-restaurant, with compostable tableware and daily-changing menus that might mean delicately dressed fig-and-goat's-cheese salad, mango-and-cucumber soup or spiced chickpeas with fragrant rice. It's mostly takeaway, with neighbours popping in and out, but there's a communal table if you want to eat in. (📞637 990078; www.lestresalacuina.com; Carrer de Sant Lluís 35; 2-/3-course menú €8.50/10; 🕐1-4pm Mon-Fri; 📷; Ⓜ Joanic)

Bar Bodega Quimet TAPAS €

9 MAP P136, B6

A relic from a bygone age, now lovingly managed by a pair of brothers, this is a delightfully atmospheric spot, with old bottles lining the walls, marble tables, tiled floors and a burnished wooden bar backed by house-vermouth barrels. The lengthy tapas list specialises in *conserves* (canned seafood), but also turns out cheese platters and fresh anchovies and octopus. (📞 93 218 41 89; Carrer de Vic 23; tapas €3-12; 🕐 10am-midnight Mon-Fri, noon-4pm & 6.30pm-late Sat & Sun; Ⓜ Fontana)

Lluritu
SEAFOOD €€

10 ✖ MAP P136, C3

From salted sardines to king prawns and razor clams, perfectly grilled, unadorned bites fresh from the ocean are the order of the day at this self-styled *desenfadada* (casual) seafood restaurant. Prized ingredients for the short, select menu are sourced from all along the Spanish coast but especially Catalonia. (📞 93 855 38 66; www.lluritu.com; Carrer del Torrent de les Flors 71; dishes €5-15; 🕐 1-4pm & 7.30-8.30pm Wed & Thu, to 12.30am Fri & Sat, noon-11.30pm Sun; Ⓜ Joanic)

Roig Robí
CATALAN €€€

11 ✖ MAP P136, B6

At this long-running altar to refined traditional cooking, the seasonally changing menu serves as a showcase for beautifully presented creations with local and organic ingredients. Dishes may include sautéed wild mushrooms to start, followed by outstanding seafood rice dishes, salt-baked market-fresh fish or slow-roasted Pyrenees lamb. Book ahead for a table on the vine-draped back patio. (📞 93 218 92 22; www.roigrobi.com; Carrer de Sèneca 20; mains €21-36; 🕐 1.30-4pm & 8.30-11.30pm Mon-Fri, 8.30-11.30pm Sat, closed 2 weeks Aug; Ⓜ Diagonal)

Les Filles
CAFE €€

12 ✖ MAP P136, C6

Both gorgeous design space and buzzing garden cafe-restaurant, Les Filles is adorned with pine-green booths, vases of fresh flowers and jazzy cushions and rugs. Rooted in fresh, seasonal flavours and organic ingredients, dishes take a health-focused turn, with options including wild-salmon pasta, quinoa bowls, creative breakfasts and cold-press juices. (📞 93 787 99 69; www.lesfillesbarcelona.com; Carrer de Minerva 2; mains €12-17; 🕐 9am-11pm Mon-Fri, from 10am Sat & Sun; 🍴; Ⓜ Diagonal)

Drinking

Bobby Gin
COCKTAIL BAR

13 🍸 MAP P136, C5

With more than 80 varieties, this whitewashed stone-walled bar is a haven for gin lovers, and arguably Barcelona's top spot for a perfectly mixed, artfully garnished, goblet-sized G&T. Try an infusion-based concoction (€10 to €12), such as citrus-infused Nordés, or a cocktail like the L'Aperitiu Modernista, with cardamom bitters and thistle liqueur. (📞 93 368 18 92; www.bobbygin.com; Carrer de Francisco Giner 47; 🕐 5pm-2am Sun-Thu, to 3am Fri & Sat; 📶; Ⓜ Diagonal)

El Ciclista

COCKTAIL BAR

14 MAP P136, C5

As the name suggests, this elegant little cocktail bar is Barcelona's original cycle-themed boozy hang-out – expect bike-wheel chandeliers and tables, handlebar pieces, and bicycle frames on the walls. Among the list of classic cocktails is an excellent selection of gin and tonics, as well as plenty of flavoured mojitos. There's often live music on Thursdays or Fridays. (☏93 368 53 02; www.elciclistabar. com; Carrer de Mozart 18; ⊗7.30pm-2am Mon-Thu, to 3am Fri & Sat; MDiagonal)

SlowMov

COFFEE

15 MAP P136, B6

SlowMov founders Carmen and François work directly with coffee producers to responsibly source their seasonal, single-origin beans, which are roasted on-site at this light-flooded cafe with original floral-tiled floors, shared tables and local artwork. Laptop workers gather for flat whites (€2.50), coffee events are organised, and organic wines, coffees, oils and jams line the shelves. (☏93 667 27 15; www.slowmov.com; Carrer de Luis Antúnez 18; ⊗8.30am-3pm Tue-Fri, 10am-2pm Sat; ⊛; MDiagonal)

Bunkers del Carmel viewpoint (p138)

BORUT TRDINA/GETTY IMAGES ©

The Changing Fortunes of Catalonia

Catalan identity is a multifaceted phenomenon, but Catalans are, more than anything else, united by the collective triumphs and shared grievances of the region's tumultuous past.

The Catalan golden age began in the early 12th century when Ramon Berenguer III, who already controlled Catalonia and parts of southern France, launched the region's first seagoing fleet. In 1137 his successor, Ramon Berenguer IV, was betrothed to Petronila, the one-year-old heiress to the Aragonese throne, thereby giving Catalonia sufficient power to expand its empire out into the Mediterranean. By the end of the 13th century, Catalan rule extended to the Balearic Islands and Catalonia's seaborne trade brought riches.

But weakened by a decline in trade and foreign battles, Catalonia became vulnerable. And when Fernando became king of Aragón in 1479 and married Isabel, Queen of Castile, Catalonia became a province of Castile. Catalonia resented its new subordinate status but could do little to overturn it. After backing the losing side in the War of the Spanish Succession (1702–13), Barcelona rose up against the Spanish crown whose armies besieged the city from March 1713 until 11 September 1714. The victorious Felipe V abolished Catalan self-rule, built a huge fort (the Ciutadella) to watch over the city, banned writing and teaching in the Catalan language, and farmed out Catalonia's colonies to other European powers.

Trade again flourished from Barcelona in the following centuries, and by the late 19th and early 20th centuries there were growing calls for greater self-governance to go with the city's burgeoning economic power. However, after Spanish general Francisco Franco's civil war victory in 1939, Catalan Francoists and the dictator's army shot in purges at least 35,000 people, most of whom were anti-Franco or presumed to be so. Over time, the use of Catalan in public was banned, all street and town names were changed into Spanish, and Castilian Spanish was the only permitted language in schools and the media. Franco's lieutenants remained in control of the city until his death in 1975 and the sense of grievance remains – though today it's directed against the central government in Madrid. Pride in Catalan culture has never been greater and, following an unsuccessful attempt by Catalonia to declare independence in 2017, the region's drive for more autonomy, or, increasingly, full independence, from Spain continues to dominate the Spanish political landscape.

Elephanta   COCKTAIL BAR

16 ⊕ MAP P136, C4

Off Gràcia's main drag, this petite
cocktail bar has an old-fashioned
feel, with plush green banquettes,
art-lined walls and a five-seat bar
with vintage stools. Gin (€8 to
€12) is the drink of choice. Snacks
include hummus, *empanades* and
torrades (toast with toppings;
€3 to €5). (🗗93 237 69 06; www.
elephanta.cat; Carrer del Torrent d'En
Vidalet 37; ⊙6pm-1.30am Mon-Thu,
to 3am Fri & Sat, to 12.30am Sun; 🛜;
ⓂJoanic)

El Rabipelao   COCKTAIL BAR

17 ⊕ MAP P136, C4

With DJs spinning salsa beats,
occasional live music and a
covered back patio, El Rabi is a cel-
ebratory space. Silent films play,
red-washed walls are decorated
with vintage photos, and there's a
colourful mural above the bar. Gins
and Caribbean rums and tropical
cocktails (€6 to €10) like mojitos
and caipirinhas pair with Venezue-
lan snacks such as *arepas* (filled
cornbread patties). (🗗93 182 50
35; www.elrabipelao.com; Carrer del
Torrent d'En Vidalet 22; ⊙7pm-1.30am
Mon-Thu, to 3am Fri & Sat, 1-4.30pm &
7pm-1.30am Sun; ⓂJoanic)

Viblioteca   WINE BAR

18 ⊕ MAP P136, C4

A glass cabinet piled high with ripe
cheese (over 50 varieties), sourced
from small-scale European producers, entices you into this small,

white, cleverly designed contemporary space. The real speciality
at Viblioteca, however, is wine, and
you can choose from 150 mostly
local labels, many of them available
by the glass. (🗗93 284 42 02; www.
viblioteca.com; Carrer de Vallfogona 12;
⊙7pm-midnight; ⓂFontana)

La Vermu   BAR

19 ⊕ MAP P136, B5

House-made *negre* (black) and
blanc (white) vermouth (€2 to €3),
served with a slice of orange and an
olive, is the speciality of this stylish
neighbourhood bar. The airy space
with exposed timber beams, red
trim and industrial lighting centres
on a marble bar. Vermouth aside,
it also has a small, stellar wine
list and smartly presented tapas.
(🗗695 925012; www.facebook.com/
lavermubcn; Carrer de Sant Domènec 15;
⊙6.30pm-midnight Mon-Thu, 12.30pm-
12.30am Fri-Sun; 🚋FGC Gràcia)

La Nena   CAFE

20 ⊕ MAP P136, C4

At this delightfully chaotic cafe,
indulge in cups of *suïssos* (rich
hot chocolate) served with heavy
homemade whipped cream and
melindros (spongy sweet biscuits),
desserts, cakes and a few savoury
dishes (including crêpes). The
place is filled with old-fashioned
photos, toys and board games.
(🗗93 285 14 76; https://la-nena-
chocolate-cafe.business.site; Carrer de
Ramón y Cajal 36; ⊙8.30am-10.30pm
Mon-Fri, from 9am Sat, from 9.30am
Sun; 👶; ⓂFontana)

Festa Major de Gràcia

During the popular week-long **Festa Major de Gràcia** (www.festamajordegracia.org), held around 15 August, locals compete for the most elaborately decorated street. Free outdoor concerts, street fairs and other events such as *correfocs* (fire runs) and *castells* (human towers) are all part of the fun.

La Vermuteria del Tano BAR

21 🚇 MAP P136, D4

Scarcely changed in decades, with barrels on the walls, old fridges with wooden doors, vintage clocks and marble-topped tables, this corner vermouth bar is a favourite local gathering point. Its house-speciality Perucchi is served traditionally with a glass of carbonated water. Tapas are also classic. Cash only! (☎93 213 10 58; www.facebook.com/VermuteriaTano; Carrer de Joan Blanques 17; ⏱9am-9pm Tue-Fri, noon-4pm Sat & Sun; 🚇Joanic)

Entertainment

Soda Acústic LIVE MUSIC

22 ⭐ MAP P136, C4

One of Gràcia's most innovative performance spaces, this low-lit modern venue stages an eclectic line-up of bands, artists and jams: jazz, world music, Balkan swing, Latin rhythms and plenty of experimental, not-easily-classifiable musicians all receive their due. (☎93 016 55 90; www.soda.cat; Carrer de les Guilleries 6; tickets free-€5; ⏱8.30pm-2.30am Wed, Thu & Sun, 9pm-3am Fri & Sat; 🚇Fontana)

La Muriel GALLERY

Set in a stylishly converted garage, this forward-thinking multi-purpose space encompasses a cultural centre, a restaurant and an events area, hosting stand-up comedy, changing exhibitions, live music on weekends and even podcast-recording sessions. (Carrer de Verntallat 30; admission free; ⏱9am-11pm Wed & Thu, to midnight Fri, noon-midnight Sat, to 11pm Sun; 🚇Lesseps)

Shopping

Colmillo de Morsa FASHION & ACCESSORIES

23 🔒 MAP P136, B6

Javier Blanco and Elisabet Vallecillo, who have made waves at Madrid's Cibeles Fashion Week, showcase their Barcelona-made women's designs at this flagship boutique-workshop filled with delicate dresses, jumpsuits and shirts in soothing tones. Fabrics are sustainably produced using nontoxic dyes, and they've also opened the floor to other up-and-coming local labels. (www.colmillodemorsa.com; Carrer de Vic 15; ⏱11am-2.30pm & 4.30-7pm Mon-Fri, 11am-2.30pm Sat; 🚉FGC Gràcia)

Casa Atlântica   CERAMICS

24 🔒 MAP P136, D5

The delicate basketry and beautiful custom-designed bowls, mugs, plant pots, vases and other ceramics dotting this charming studio-boutique are created by Galician artisans Belén and Lester, who collaborate with small-scale, family-owned village workshops across Galicia and Portugal to keep traditional crafts alive. (📞93 382 18 88; www.casaatlantica.es; Carrer de la Llibertat 7; ⏰noon-8.30pm Mon-Sat; Ⓜ️Diagonal)

Fromagerie Can Luc   CHEESE

25 🔒 MAP P136, B5

At any given time, this inviting shop stocks 150 different varieties of European cheese. Catalan favourites are the speciality, though you'll also spot a selection from France, Italy, the Netherlands, Switzerland and Britain. Wines, condiments, crackers and cheese knives are available too, along with gourmet picnic hampers (€25 to €100) and tasting sets. (📞93 007 47 83; www.canluc.es; Carrer de Berga 4; ⏰5-9pm Mon, 10am-2.30pm & 5-8.30pm Tue-Sat; Ⓡ FGC Gràcia)

Amalia Vermell   JEWELLERY

26 🔒 MAP P136, B5

Striking geometric jewellery made from high-quality materials such as sterling silver is hand-crafted right here in the atelier by designer-owner Pamela Masfer-rer, who also offers long-term jewellery-making workshops. Browse for pendants, necklaces, bracelets and rings, as well as vibrant homeware pieces and dresses by Barcelona brands. (📞655 754008; www.amaliavermell.com; Carrer del Planeta 11; ⏰5-9pm Mon-Thu, 10.30am-2.30pm & 5-9pm Fri & Sat, hours can vary; Ⓜ️Fontana)

Bodega Bonavista   WINE

27 🔒 MAP P136, C6

An excellent little neighbourhood bodega, Bonavista endeavours to seek out great wines at reasonable prices. The stock is mostly from Catalonia and elsewhere in Spain, but there's also a well-chosen French selection. The Bonavista also doubles as a deli, with some especially good cheeses. You can sample wines by the glass, along with cheeses and charcuterie, at the in-store tables. (📞93 218 81 99; www.facebook.com/bodegabonavistabcn; Carrer de Bonavista 10; ⏰10am-2.30pm & 5-9pm Mon-Fri, noon-3pm & 6-9pm Sat; Ⓜ️Fontana)

Hibernian   BOOKS

28 🔒 MAP P136, B4

Barcelona's biggest second-hand English bookshop stocks thousands of titles covering all sorts of subjects, from cookery to children's classics. (📞93 217 47 96; www.hibernianbooks.com; Carrer de Montseny 17; ⏰4-8.30pm Mon, 10.30am-8.30pm Tue-Sat; Ⓜ️Fontana)

Explore

Montjuïc, Poble Sec & Sant Antoni

Best reached by soaring cable car, the hillside overlooking the port hosts some of the city's finest art collections, plus gardens, an imposing castle and fabulous views. Just below Montjuïc lie the lively tapas bars and sloping streets of Poble Sec, while the newly fashionable neighbourhood of Sant Antoni draws a stylish young crowd.

The Short List

○ **Museu Nacional d'Art de Catalunya (MNAC; p148)** Dedicating a day to the world's most important collection of early-medieval art in the Romanesque halls and six centuries of Catalan art.

○ **Fundació Joan Miró (p150)** Viewing brilliant works from one of the art world's giants, inside the light-filled galleries designed by Josep Lluís Sert.

○ **Sant Antoni Stroll (p154 & 158)** Wandering between vintage-chic coffee shops, creative tapas bars and a 19th-century market in this revitalised neighbourhood.

○ **CaixaForum (p158)** Catching a ground-breaking art exhibition in a Modernista former factory.

○ **Telefèric del Port (p161)** Gazing out over the city on a cable-car ride between Barceloneta and Montjuïc.

Getting There & Around

Ⓜ Stops: Espanya, Poble Sec, Paral·lel, Sant Antoni.

🚌 Buses 150 and 55 serve Montjuïc.

🚋 Funicular from Paral·lel to Parc Montjuïc.

🚋 There are two cable cars up to Montjuic.

Neighbourhood Map on p156

Castell de Montjuïc (p153) GYPSYPICTURESHOW/SHUTTERSTOCK ©

Top Experience 📷

Take in the masterpieces of Museu Nacional d'Art de Catalunya

The spectacular neobaroque silhouette of the Palau Nacional can be seen from across the city. Built for the 1929 World Exhibition and restored in 2005, MNAC houses a vast collection of mostly Catalan art spanning the early Middle Ages to the early 20th century. The high point is the collection of Roman-esque frescoes, considered the most important concentration of early medieval art in the world.

◎ MAP P156, C4

www.museunacional.cat

Mirador del Palau Nacional, Parc de Montjuïc

adult/child €12/free, after 3pm Sat & 1st Sun of month free; ⏱ hours vary

Romanesque Masterpieces

Rescued from neglected country churches across northern Catalonia in the early 20th century, the Romanesque collection consists of 21 frescoes, woodcarvings and painted altar frontals. The insides of several churches have been recreated and the frescoes placed as they were when in situ. Most striking are the magnificent image of Christ in Majesty done around 1123, taken from the Església de Sant Climent de Taüll in the Vall de Boí (Sala 7), and the frescoes of the Virgin Mary and Christ Child in the nearby Església de Santa Maria de Taüll (Sala 9).

Gothic Collection

Opposite the Romanesque collection, the Gothic art section has Catalan Gothic painting and works from other Spanish and Mediterranean regions. Look out especially for the work of Bernat Martorell in Sala 32 and Jaume Huguet in Sala 34.

Renaissance & Baroque

Next you pass into the 2018-launched Renaissance & Baroque gallery, which exhibits some 300 pieces including works by Diego Velázquez, Francisco de Zurbarán, Josep de Ribera, Francisco Goya, Tiepolo, Rubens, El Greco and Canaletto. Incorporated into this section are two excellent private collections, the Cambò Bequest by Francesc Cambó and the Thyssen-Bornemisza collection on loan by Madrid's Museo Thyssen-Bornemisza.

Modern Catalan Art

An early Salvador Dalí painting, *Retrat del meu pare* (Portrait of My Father), Juan Gris' collage-like paintings, the brilliant portraits of Marià Fortuny, and 1930s call-to-arms posters against the Francoist onslaught are among the top-floor highlights. There are also works by Ramon Casas, Santiago Rusiñol, Antoni Tàpies and Antoni Gaudí.

★ **Top Tips**

o Save money by purchasing the Airticket BCN, a €35 pass that provides admission to six museums (including the MNAC).

o Be sure to take in the fine city view from the **terrace** (Passeig de Santa Madrona 39-41; 🚌55) just in front of the museum, which draws crowds around sunset.

o Another fine viewpoint is the museum's roof terrace (included in admission or €2 if you only want to visit the rooftop).

✕ **Take a Break**

There's a casual cafe on the museum's main level, plus a seasonal terrace, for drinks, sandwiches and desserts.

Alternatively, wander 10 minutes down into Poble Sec to Barcelona's favourite Italian restaurant Xemei (p163).

★ **Getting There**

🚌55, Ⓜ Espanya

Top Experience 📷

See Miró's best at Fundació Joan Miró

Joan Miró, the city's best-known 20th-century artistic progeny, bequeathed this art foundation to his home town in 1971. The light-filled buildings, designed by close friend and architect Josep Lluís Sert (who also built Miró's Mallorca studios), are crammed with seminal works, from Miró's earliest timid sketches to paintings from his last years.

◎ MAP P156, E4

📞 93 443 94 70

www.fmirobcn.org

Avinguda de Miramar

adult/child €13/free, multimedia guide €5

🕐 hours vary

🚌 55, 150, 🚋 from Paral·lel

Sert's Temple to Miró's Art

Sert's shimmering white temple to one of Spain's artistic luminaries is considered one of the world's most outstanding museum buildings. The architect designed it after spending many of Franco's dictatorship years in the USA as head of the School of Design at Harvard University. The foundation rests amid the greenery of the mountains and holds the greatest single collection of Miró's work, including around 220 of his paintings, 180 sculptures, some textiles and more than 8000 drawings spanning his entire life. Only a small portion is ever on display, interspersed with courtyards, water features and olive trees.

The Collection

Just inside the entrance, you'll find Sala 1, the Sala Joan Prats, with works spanning the early years until 1919. Here you can see how the young Miró moved from relative realism towards his own unique style that uses primary colours and morphed shapes symbolising the moon, the female form and birds.

Sala 2, the Sala Pilar Juncosa (after Miró's wife), covers his surrealist years (1925–68). Sala 3 contains masterworks from the 1960s and 1970s, such as *Personatge Davant del Sol*. Salas 5, 6 and 7 host a selection of the private Katsuta collection of Miró works from 1914 to 1971. Sala 9 exhibits some more major paintings and bronzes from the 1960s onwards, including the famed 1970s *antipintura* works.

Next up, Sala 11 holds *Tapís de la Fundació*, a giant tapestry in Miró's trademark primary colours. You'll then pass *Mercury Fountain (Font de Mercur)* by Alexander Calder, a rebuilt work that was originally created for the 1937 Paris Fair.

★ Top Tips

o For the full experience, pay the extra €5 for the multimedia guide, which includes commentary on major works, additional info on Miro's life and work, and images and photographs.

o Arrive at opening times for the smallest crowds.

o Outside on the eastern flank of the museum lies the Jardí de les Escultures, a small garden with modern sculpture.

✖ Take a Break

Near the centre of the museum, a light-filled cafe-restaurant serves freshly prepared Mediterranean dishes. The adjoining outdoor terrace is a fine spot for a drink.

A 500m walk east of the museum (head left when exiting), Salts Montjuïc (p153) has tapas, drinks and fabulous city views.

Walking Tour 🥾

Montjuïc's Gardens & Panoramas

Looming above the port, sloping Montjuïc is best explored on foot, along the numerous forest paths that zigzag through gardens and skirt the various exciting sights. The key here is planning: there's far too much to see in one day! This itinerary takes in the area's finest viewpoints and green spaces.

Walk Facts

Start Castell de Montjuïc; 🚠 Castell de Montjuïc

End Jardins de Joan Maragall; Ⓜ Plaça Espanya

Length 3km; 1½ hours

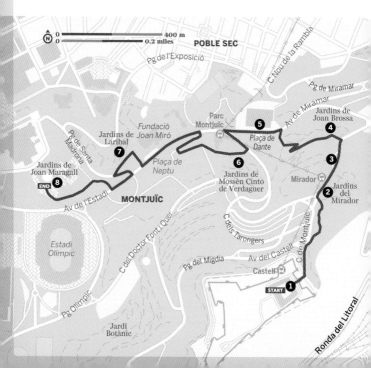

❶ Castell de Montjuïc

Get the Telefèric de Montjuïc cable car to the hilltop **Castell de Montjuïc** (p158); its dark history is today overshadowed by the stupendous views over Barcelona. Don't miss the sea-facing trail behind the fortress.

❷ Jardins del Mirador

A short stroll northeast down the shaded Camí del Mar pedestrian trail leads to another inspiring viewpoint over the city and sea at the **Jardins del Mirador** (www.barcelona.cat; Carretera de Montjuïc; admission free; ⏱10am-sunset; 🚠Telefèric de Montjuïc, Mirador), opposite the Mirador cable car station.

❸ Plaça de la Sardana

Immediately downhill, **Plaça de la Sardana** (Carrer de Montjuïc; 🚌150) is decorated with a sculpture of people engaged in the classic Catalan folk dance.

❹ Jardins de Joan Brossa

To the left of the square lie the charming landscaped **Jardins de Joan Brossa** (www.barcelona.cat; Plaça de la Sardana; admission free; ⏱10am-sunset; 🚠Telefèric de Montjuïc, Mirador), with fine views from the site of a former amusement park, now covered in Mediterranean species from cypresses to olive trees to large-fan palms.

❺ Salts Montjuïc

Take a break with a view at all-day terrace tapas bar **Salts Montjuïc** (📞616 893356; www.saltsmontjuic.com; Avinguda de Miramar 31; ⏱10am-midnight Sun-Thu, to 1am Fri & Sat; 🚌55, 150), overlooking Montjuïc's municipal pools (with a €25 evening swim-and-dine deal available!).

❻ Jardins de Mossèn Cinto de Verdaguer

Cross Carrer dels Tarongers to the painstakingly laid out **Jardins de Mossèn Cinto de Verdaguer** (www.barcelona.cat; Avinguda de Miramar 30; admission free; ⏱10am-sunset; 🚌55, 150), home to 80,000 bulbs: tulips, narcissus, crocus, dahlia, lotus flowers, water lilies.

❼ Jardins de Laribal

Just beyond the **Fundació Joan Miró** (p150), the soothing terraced gardens of the 1922-opened **Jardins de Laribal** (www.barcelona.cat; Passeig de Santa Madrona 2; admission free; ⏱10am-sunset; 🚌55) are linked by paths, stairs and wisteria-clad walkways. Pretty sculpted watercourses take inspiration from Granada's Alhambra.

❽ Jardins de Joan Maragall

Continue 300m west to reach the little-visited, weekend-only **Jardins de Joan Maragall** (www.barcelona.cat; Avinguda dels Montanyans 48; admission free; ⏱10am-3pm Sat & Sun; Ⓜ Plaça Espanya) with ornamental fountains and a neo-classical palace (the Spanish royal family's residence in Barcelona).

Walking Tour 🥾

Nightlife in Sant Antoni & Poble Sec

The area of Poble Sec (literally 'Dry Town'!) and neighbouring Sant Antoni is a current hot destination, with a buzzing, growing array of chic cafes, creative bars, clubs, boutiques and new-wave restaurants. It seems now everyone wants to live in this once-sleepy corner of Barcelona.

Walk Facts

Start Bar Ramón;
Ⓜ Sant Antoni

End Sala Apolo;
Ⓜ Paral·lel

Length 2.1km; as long as you like!

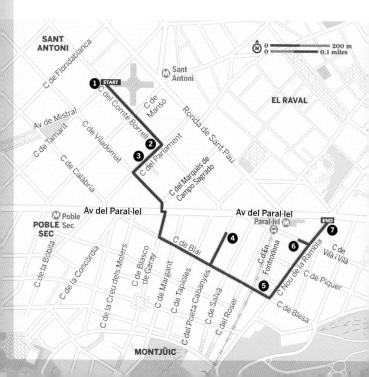

❶ Bar Ramón

Bar Ramón (☎93 325 02 83; http://barramon.dudaone.com; Carrer del Comte Borrell 81; tapas €5-12; ⏰8.30-11.30pm Mon-Thu, 2-4pm & 8.30-11.30pm Fri & Sat; Ⓜ Sant Antoni) is a much-loved blues-filled joint for superb tapas: cured ham, grilled prawns, house-speciality *jabuguitos* (chorizo in cider with Cabrales-cheese sauce).

❷ Federal

On Sant Antoni's main stretch Australian-founded **Federal** (☎93 187 36 07; www.federalcafe.es; Carrer del Parlament 39; mains €7-12; ⏰8am-11.30pm Mon-Thu, to midnight Fri, 9am-midnight Sat, 9am-5.30pm Sun; 📶🚼; Ⓜ Sant Antoni) offers expertly crafted coffee, evening cocktails and creative brunches.

❸ Bar Calders

At weekends, neighbourhood fave **Bar Calders** (☎93 329 93 49; Carrer del Parlament 25; ⏰5pm-2am Mon-Thu, to 2.30am Fri, 11am-2.30am Sat, 11am-12.30am Sun; Ⓜ Poble Sec) is unbeatable as an all-day cafe, tapas, wine and vermouth bar; the outdoor tables are the go-to meeting point for Sant Antoni's boho set.

❹ El Rouge

Decadence is the word that springs to mind at bordello-red cocktail lounge **El Rouge** (☎634 127581; www.facebook.com/elrougebar; Carrer del Poeta Cabanyes 21; ⏰9pm-2.30am Wed-Thu & Sun, to 3am Fri & Sat; 📶; Ⓜ Paral·lel). You can sometimes catch DJs, risqué poetry soirées, cabaret shows, jam sessions or tango.

❺ Gran Bodega Saltó

The ranks of barrels and classic tapas tell the century-old history at **Gran Bodega Saltó** (☎93 441 37 09; www.bodegasalto.net; Carrer de Blesa 36; ⏰6pm-1am Mon-Thu, noon-3am Fri & Sat, noon-midnight Sun). Now it gets busy during live-music sessions.

❻ Abirradero

Buzzing **Abirradero** (☎93 461 94 46; www.abirradero.com; Carrer de Vilà i Vilà 77; ⏰noon-midnight Sun-Thu, to 2am Fri & Sat; 📶) is one of Barcelona's best craft breweries, with 40 of its own beers rotating on the taps.

❼ Sala Apolo

The iconic, velvet-clad **Sala Apolo** (☎93 441 40 01; www.sala-apolo.com; Carrer Nou de la Rambla 113; club incl drink from €15; ⏰concerts from 8pm, club from midnight; Ⓜ Paral·lel) is a fine old theatre turned club where you feel as though you're on a movie set. Evening concerts give way to DJs post-midnight.

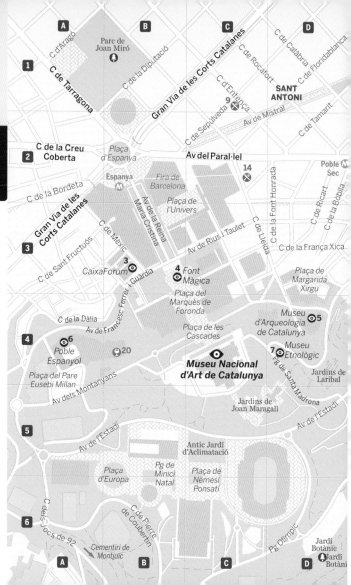

A
B
C
D

1

C d'Aragó

Parc de
Joan Miró

C de Tarragona

C de la Diputació

Gran Via de les Corts Catalanes

C de Calàbria

C de Rocafort

C de Floridablanca

C d'Entença

9

SANT
ANTONI

C de Sepúlveda

Av de Mistral

C de Tamarit

2

C de la Creu
Coberta

Plaça
d'Espanya

Av del Paral·lel

Poble
Sec

14

Espanya

Fira de
Barcelona

C de la Bordeta

C de la Font Honrada

C de Ricart

C de la Bòbila

Gran Via de les
Corts Catalanes

C de Mèxic

Plaça de
l'Univers

Av de la Reina
Maria Cristina

Plaça de
Margarida
Xirgu

3

C de Sant Fructuós

Av de Rius i Taulet

C de Lleida

C de la França Xica

CaixaForum **3**

4 Font
Màgica

C de Francesc Ferrer i Guàrdia

Plaça del
Marquès de
Foronda

Museu
d'Arqueologia
de Catalunya **5**

C de la Dàlia

Av de Francesc Ferrer i Guàrdia

Plaça de les
Cascades

Museu
Etnològic **7**

4

6
Poble
Espanyol

20

Museu Nacional
d'Art de Catalunya

Pg de Santa Madrona

Jardins de
Laribal

Plaça del Pare
Eusebi Millan

Av dels Montanyans

Jardins de
Joan Maragall

Av de l'Estadi

5

Av de l'Estadi

Antic Jardí
d'Aclimatació

Plaça
d'Europa

Pg de
Minici
Natal

Plaça de
Nèmesi
Ponsatí

C dels Jocs de 92

C de Pierre
de Coubertin

Pg Olímpic

Jardí
Botànic

Jardí
Botàni

6

Cementiri de
Montjuïc

A
B
C
D

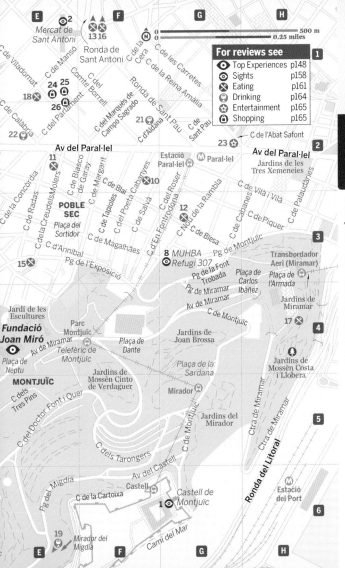

E
2
Mercat de
Sant Antoni
13 16
F

G

H

500 m
0.25 miles

Ronda de
Sant Antoni

C de Viladomat

C de Manso

C de la Cera

C de les Carretes

C de la Reina Amàlia

For reviews see

1

	Top Experiences	p148
	Sights	p158
	Eating	p161
	Drinking	p164
	Entertainment	p165
	Shopping	p165

Comte Borrell

C del Marquès de
Campo Sagrado

Ronda de
Sant Pau

24 25

26

18

C de Calàbria

C del Parlament

21

C d'Aldana

C de
Sant Pau

22

23

C de l'Abat Safont

2

Av del Paral·lel

Av del Paral·lel

Estació
Paral·lel

Paral·lel

Jardins de les
Tres Xemeneies

11

C de Blasco
de Garay

C de Margarit

C de Blai

10

C del Roser

C de la Rambla

C de Vila i Vilà

C de Palaudàries

POBLE
SEC

C de la Concòrdia

C de Radas

C de la Creu dels Molers

C del Poeta Cabanyes

C de Tapioles

C de Salvà

C de Magalhães

C d'En Fontrodona

12

C Nou de la Rambla

C de Blesa

C de Cabanes

C de Piquer

3

Plaça del
Sortidor

C d'Annibal

Pg de l'Exposició

15

8 MUHBA
Refugi 307

Pg de Montjuïc

Transbordador
Aeri (Miramar)

Pg de la Font
Trobada

Plaça de
Carlos
Ibáñez

Plaça de
l'Armada

Jardí de les
Escultures

**Fundació
Joan Miró**

Pg de Miramar

Av de Miramar

C de Montjuïc

Jardins de
Miramar

17

4

Parc
Montjuïc

Plaça de
Neptú

Av de Miramar

Telefèric de
Montjuïc

Plaça de
Dante

Jardins de
Joan Brossa

Jardins de
Mossèn Costa
i Llobera

MONTJUÏC

C dels
Tres Pins

Jardins de
Mossèn Cinto
de Verdaguer

Plaça de la
Sardana

Mirador

C del Doctor Font i Quer

Jardins del
Mirador

Ctra de Miramar

Ctra de Miramar

Ronda del Litoral

5

C dels Tarongers

C de Montjuïc

Pg del Migdia

Av del Castell

Castell

C de la Cartoixa

Castell de
Montjuïc

1

Estació
del Port

6

19

Mirador del
Migdia

Camí del Mar

E

F

G

H

Sights

Castell de Montjuïc FORTRESS

1 ◉ MAP P156, G6

Enjoying commanding views over the Mediterranean, this forbidding fortress dominates the southeastern heights of Montjuïc. It dates, in its present form, from the late 17th and 18th centuries, though there's been a watchtower here since 1073. For most of its dark history, it has been used as a political prison and killing ground. Anarchists were executed here around the end of the 19th century, fascists during the civil war and Republicans after it – most notoriously Republican Catalan president Lluís Companys in 1940. (📞 93 256 44 40; https://ajuntament.barcelona. cat; Carretera de Montjuïc 66; adult/child €5/3, after 3pm Sun & 1st Sun of month free; 🕙 10am-8pm Mar-Oct, to 6pm Nov-Feb; 🚌 150, 🚠 Telefèric de Montjuïc, Castell de Montjuïc)

Mercat de Sant Antoni MARKET

2 ◉ MAP P156, E1

Just beyond the western edge of El Raval, this glorious iron-and-brick market was originally completed in 1882, but reopened in 2018 with 250 stalls following a nine-year renovation job. It's a great place to stock up on seasonal produce or grab a bite in between browsing the fashion, textiles and homewares stalls. Also on display are the remains of a piece of the Roman Via Augusta

and a 1st-century-CE mausoleum, as well as a ruined 17th-century defensive wall. (📞 93 426 35 21; www.mercatdesantantoni.com; Carrer del Comte d'Urgell 1; 🕙 8am-8.30pm Mon-Sat; Ⓜ Sant Antoni)

CaixaForum GALLERY

3 ◉ MAP P156, B3

The La Caixa building society prides itself on its involvement in (and ownership of) art, in particular all that is contemporary. The bank's premier expo space in Barcelona hosts part of its extensive global collection, as well as fascinating temporary international exhibitions, in the completely renovated former Casaramona factory, an outstanding brick Modernista creation by Josep Puig i Cadafalch. (📞 93 476 86 00; www.caixaforum.es; Avinguda de Francesc Ferrer i Guàrdia 6-8; adult/child €4/free, 1st Sun of month free; 🕙 10am-8pm year-round, to 11pm Wed Jul & Aug; Ⓜ Espanya)

Font Màgica FOUNTAIN

4 ◉ MAP P156, B3

Originally created for the 1929 World Exposition, this huge colour-lit fountain has again been a magnet since the 1992 Olympics, shimmering on the long sweep of Avinguda de la Reina Maria Cristina to the grand Palau Nacional. With a flourish, the 'Magic Fountain' erupts into a feast of musical, backlit aquatic life; it's a unique 15-minute night performance. (Avinguda de la Reina

Maria Cristina; admission free; ⊙every 30min 9.30-10.30pm Wed-Sun Jun-Sep, 9-10pm Thu-Sat Apr, May & Oct, 8-9pm Thu-Sat Nov-Mar; Ⓜ Espanya)

Museu d'Arqueologia de Catalunya

MUSEUM

5 ⊙ MAP P156, D4

Occupying the 1929 World Exhibition's Graphic Arts Palace, this intriguing archaeology museum covers both Catalonia and cultures from across Spain. There's good material on the Balearic Islands (including 5th- to 3rd-century-BCE statues of Phoenician goddess Tanit from Ibiza) and the Greek and Roman city of Empúries (Emporion), as well as the region's prehistoric inhabitants. Don't miss the 53,200-year-old human jaw found near Sitges, or the beautiful Roman mosaic depicting Les Tres Gràcies (The Three Graces), unearthed in the 18th century. (MAC; ☎ 93 423 21 49; www.macbarcelona.cat; Passeig de Santa Madrona 39-41; adult/child €6/free; ⊙9.30am-7pm Tue-Sat, 10am-2.30pm Sun; ☒55, Ⓜ Poble Sec)

Poble Espanyol

CULTURAL CENTRE

6 ⊙ MAP P156, A4

Welcome to Spain! All of it! This 'Spanish Village' is an intriguing scrapbook of Spanish architecture built for the local-crafts section of the 1929 World Exhibition. You can meander from Andalucía to Galicia in the space of a couple of hours, visiting surprisingly good to-scale copies of Spain's characteristic structures. The 117 buildings

Poble Espanyol

include restaurants, cafes, bars and clubs, and craft shops and workshops. (☑93 508 63 00; www.poble-espanyol.com; Avinguda de Francesc Ferrer i Guàrdia 13; adult/child €14/7; ⏲9am-8pm Mon, to midnight Tue-Thu & Sun, to 3am Fri, to 4am Sat; ⌕13, 23, 150, Ⓜ Espanya)

Museu Etnològic MUSEUM

7 ◉ MAP P156, D4

Delving into Catalonia's rich heritage, Barcelona's ethnology museum presents an intriguing permanent display from its 70,000-object collection, with multilanguage panels. Exhibits cover origin myths, religious festivals, folklore, and the blending of sacred and secular. There are several *gegants* (massive Catalan papier-mâché figures), including

depictions of King Jaume I and Queen Violant, and a dragon and devil costumes used in *corre-focs* (fire runs), which still figure prominently in Catalan festivals. (☑93 256 34 84; www.barcelona.cat; Passeig de Santa Madrona 16; adult/child €5/free, from 3pm Sun & 1st Sun of month free; ⏲10am-7pm Tue-Sat, to 8pm Sun; ⌕55)

MUHBA Refugi 307 HISTORIC SITE

8 ◉ MAP P156, G3

Barcelona was the city most heavily bombed by Franco's air forces during the Spanish Civil War, and as a result developed more than 1300 air-raid shelters. Now overseen by the Museu d'Història de Barcelona (MUHBA), the city's 307th refuge (one of its best preserved) was dug under a fold of

Telefèric de Montjuïc

Cable Cars

The quickest and most scenic route from the beach to the mountain is via the **Telefèric del Port** (Map p96, C8; www.telefericodebarcelona. com; Passeig de Joan de Borbó; one way/return €11/16.50; ⏱10.30am-8pm Jun-early Sep, shorter hours early Sep-May; 🚌V15, V19, Ⓜ Barceloneta) cable car, which runs between the Torre de Sant Sebastià in Barceloneta and the Miramar stop on Montjuïc. From the Parc Montjuïc cable car station on northern Montjuïc, the separate **Telefèric de Montjuïc** (Map p156, F4; www.telefericdemontjuic.cat; Avinguda de Miramar 30; adult/child one way €8.40/6.60; ⏱10am-9pm Jun-Sep, to 7pm Mar-May & Oct, to 6pm Nov-Feb; 🚌55, 150) whizzes you up to the **Castell de Montjuïc** (p158) via the mirador (lookout point).

northern Montjuïc by local citizens from 1937 to 1939. Compulsory tours (reservations essential) run on Sunday only: English at 10.30am, Spanish at 11.30am and Catalan at 12.30pm. (📞93 256 21 00; http://ajuntament.barcelona. cat; Carrer Nou de la Rambla 175; tour adult/child €3.50/free; ⏱tours 10.30am, 11.30am & 12.30pm Sun; Ⓜ Paral·lel)

Eating

Enigma
GASTRONOMY €€€

9 🍴 MAP P156, C1

Resembling a 3D art installation, this conceptual Michelin-star creation from the famed Adrià brothers is a 40-course tour de force of cutting-edge gastronomy across six dining spaces. A meal takes 3½ hours and includes customised cocktail pairings (you can order additional drinks). There's a minimum of two diners;

reserve months in advance (€100 nonrefundable deposit per guest). (📞616 696322; www.elbarri.com; Carrer de Sepúlveda 38-40; tasting menu €220; ⏱7-9.30pm Tue-Fri, 1-2.30pm & 7-9.30pm Sat; Ⓜ Espanya)

Quimet i Quimet
TAPAS €

10 🍴 MAP P156, F2

Now led by its fourth generation, family-run Quimet i Quimet has been passed down since 1914. There's barely space to swing a *calamar* (squid) in this bottle-lined, standing-room-only place, but it's a treat for the palate. Try delectable made-to-order *montaditos* (tapas on bread), such as salmon with greek yoghurt or tuna belly with sea urchin, with a house wine or vermouth. (📞93 442 31 42; www. quimetquimet.com; Carrer del Poeta Cabanyes 25; tapas €4-10, montaditos €3-4; ⏱noon-4pm & 8-10.30pm Mon-Fri, closed Aug; Ⓜ Paral·lel)

Carrer de Blai

Carrer de Blai in Poble Sec is packed with busy tapas and *pintxo* (Basque tapas) bars, both classic and contemporary, where you can feast on bite-sized batches of deliciousness at around €1 or €2 a piece – from chunks of perfectly gooey tortilla to king prawns with *piquillo* peppers.

Mano Rota   FUSION €€

11 MAP P156, E2

Exposed brick, aluminium pipes, industrial lighting and recycled timbers set a pleasingly contemporary tone for inspired bistro cooking at Mano Rota ('broken hand', a Spanish idiom for consummate skill). Asian, South American and Mediterranean flavours meet in fusion temptations such as Thai-inspired coconut-laced *suquet* (Catalan fish stew), monkfish tagine or shiso-leaf quesadillas. The 12-course tasting menu is decent value at €65. (☑93 164 80 41; www.manorota.com; Carrer de la Creu dels Molers 4; mains €13-20; ☺8-11.30pm Mon, 1-3.30pm & 8-11.30pm Tue-Sat; MPoble Sec)

Palo Cortao   TAPAS €€

12 MAP P156, G3

Chicly contemporary and welcoming Palo Cortao is renowned for its beautifully executed seafood and meat *raciones* with hints of Andalucía, accompanied by Jerez sherry and other elegant Spanish wines. Highlights include truffled-chicken cannelloni, fried aubergines with honey and miso, delicate cheese plates, and tuna tataki with *ajo blanco*. (☑93 188 90 67; www.palocortao.es; Carrer Nou de la Rambla 146; medias raciones €7-10; ☺8pm-1am Tue-Fri, 1-5pm & 8pm-1am Sat & Sun; MParal·lel)

Alkímia   CATALAN €€€

13 MAP P156, F1

Inside the innovatively redesigned Fàbrica Moritz brewery, amid tile-patterned floors and shimmering white surfaces, culinary alchemist Jordi Vilà creates refined Catalan dishes with a twist that have earned him a Michelin star: potato-and-truffle soufflé, wild fish of the day in shellfish stew, mushrooms with caramelised cabbage and carrot toffee, and other seriously original visions. (☑93 207 61 15; www.alkimia.cat; Ronda de Sant Antoni 41; mains €26-47, tasting menu €138; ☺1.30-3.30pm & 8-10.30pm Mon-Fri; MUniversitat)

Casa de Tapas Cañota   TAPAS €€

14 MAP P156, C2

This friendly, unfussy old-timer serves affordable, nicely turned out tapas plates. Seafood is the speciality, with rich razor clams, garlic-fried prawns and tender octopus. Book ahead for weekends. The Iglesias family also runs traditional seafood spot Rías de Galicia next door and Japanese-fusion Espai Kru, just upstairs. (📞93 325 91 71; www.casadetapas. com; Carrer de Lleida 7; tapas €5-15; 🕐1-4pm & 7.30pm-midnight Tue-Sat, 1-4pm Sun; Ⓜ Poble Sec)

Xemei

VENETIAN €€

15 🍴 MAP P156, E3

Everyone's favourite Italian, Xemei ('Twins' in Venetian) is a wonderful, authentically delicious slice of Venice in Barcelona, named for its twin Venetian owners Stefano and Max Colombo. To the accompaniment of gentle jazz and vintage-inspired design, you might try a light burrata salad or Venetian-fish platter, followed by *bigoli* pasta in anchovy-and-onion sauce, squid-ink spaghetti, grilled octopus or seasonal risotto. (📞93 553 51 40; www.xemei.es; Passeig de l'Exposició 85; mains €16-25; 🕐1.45-3.30pm & 8.45-11pm, closed 2 weeks Aug; Ⓜ Poble Sec)

Fàbrica Moritz

GASTROPUB €€

16 🍴 MAP P156, F1

In a building redesigned by architect Jean Nouvel, with a menu created by chef Jordi Vilà of Michelin-starred Alkímia (also on the premises), the popular Moritz brewery restaurant offers pan-European gastropub fare such as gourmet sandwiches, wood-oven-baked eggs, fish and chips, frankfurters with sauerkraut and *flammkuchen* (Alsatian-style pizza). The adjacent wine bar does tapas, vermouth and beer

tastings. (📞93 426 00 50; www. moritz.com; Ronda de Sant Antoni 41; tapas €4-10, mains €8-18; 🕐8.30am-1.30am Sun-Thu, to 2am Fri & Sat; Ⓜ Sant Antoni)

Martínez

SPANISH €€€

17 🍴 MAP P156, H4

With a fabulous panorama over the port, stylish Martínez is a standout among Montjuïc's lacklustre dining options. The terrace is ideal for warm-day lunches of the signature rice dishes. There are also oysters, calamari, fresh market fish and other seafood hits, plus cured ham and grilled meats. The bar stays open until 1.30am or 2.30am. (📞93 106 60 52; www.martinezbar celona.com; Carretera de Miramar 38; mains €20-35; 🕐1-11pm; 🚌150, 🚡Telefèric del Port, Miramar)

Quimet i Quimet (p161)

PAUL BARRON/SHUTTERSTOCK ©

Sant Antoni Gloriós
TAPAS €

18 🍴 MAP P156, E1

Launched by neighbourhood chef Fran Manduley, this smartly updated Sant Antoni bodega with oversized mirrors, wine-barrel tables and bottle-lined walls pulls in a local crowd. Tapas are unpretentious and expertly prepared, including vegetable-stuffed omelettes and charcuterie platters of truffled mortadella with Catalan cheeses. Vermouth-hour snacks include cod fritters and *patates braves*. (📞93 424 06 28; www.facebook.com/SantAntoniGlorioso; Carrer de Mansó 42; dishes €4-12; ⏱1-11pm Tue-Sat, 1-3pm Sun; Ⓜ Poble Sec)

Drinking

La Caseta del Migdia
BAR

19 🍺 MAP P156, E6

The effort of getting to what is, for all intents and purposes, a simple *xiringuito* (summer snack bar) perched atop Montjuïc's seaward slopes, is worth it. Gaze out on the Mediterranean over a beer or soft drink by day. As sunset approaches, the atmosphere changes, as reggae, samba and funk waft out over the hillside. Food is fired on outdoor grills. (📞617 956572; www.lacaseta.org; Mirador del Migdia; ⏱8pm-1am Wed-Fri, noon-1am Sat & Sun Apr-Sep, noon-sunset Sat & Sun Oct-Mar; 🚌150)

La Terrrazza
CLUB

20 🍺 MAP P156, B4

Come summer, this re-created Balearic-style mansion attracts squadrons of beautiful people, locals and visitors alike, for a full-on night of music (mainly house, techno and electronica), cocktails and vaguely Ibiza vibes. It's set partly under the stars, inside the Poble Espanyol (p159) complex. (📞687 969825; http://laterrrazza.com; Avinguda de Francesc Ferrer i Guàrdia 13, Poble Espanyol; cover €10-15; ⏱midnight-6.30am Thu-Sat May-Sep; 🚌13, 23, 150, Ⓜ Espanya)

Bar Olimpia
BAR

21 🍺 MAP P156, F2

This great little neighbourhood bar is a small slice of Barcelona history. It was here (and on the surrounding block) that the popular Olimpia Theatre Circus performed between 1924 and 1947. Today the retro setting draws a diverse crowd, who come for house-made vermouth and strong G&Ts. (📞93 129 90 93; www.facebook.com/bar.olimpia.5; Carrer d'Aldana 11; ⏱9pm-1am Mon & Tue, 7pm-1am Wed, 6pm-1am Thu, 8pm-3am Fri & Sat; Ⓜ Paral·lel)

La Mari Ollero
WINE BAR

22 🍺 MAP P156, E2

With red-brick walls and marble tables, elegant La Mari Ollero brings a buzzy contemporary spin and a jolly Andalucian touch to the classic Catalan *vermuteria*.

Wines (glass €3 to €5) come from the south (including sherry-style Montilla-Moriles) as well as Catalonia and elsewhere in northern Spain. Tapas (€1 to €6) combine flavours from Barcelona and Córdoba. (📞93 327 84 85; www.lamariollero.com; Carrer de Calàbria 5; 🕑noon-midnight, hours can vary; Ⓜ Poble Sec)

Entertainment

BARTS   LIVE PERFORMANCE

23 ⭐ MAP P156, G2

BARTS has a solid reputation for its innovative line-up of urban-dance troupes, electro swing, psychedelic pop, circus acrobatics and other eclectic shows. Its smart design combines a comfortable midsized auditorium with excellent acoustics. (Barcelona Arts on Stage; 📞93 324 84 92; www.barts.cat; Avinguda del Paral·lel 62; Ⓜ Paral·lel)

Shopping

Popcorn Store   FASHION & ACCESSORIES

24 🔒 MAP P156, E1

Cutting-edge Barcelona women's labels at this pink-patterned

boutique mean asymmetrical tops, jackets and dresses, bold prints and delicate lace. Men will find stylish shirts, trousers and belts from Italian and other European designers. (www.facebook.com/popcornstorebcn; Carrer Viladomat 30-32; 🕑11am-3pm & 4.30-8.30pm Mon-Sat)

Llibreria Calders   BOOKS

25 🔒 MAP P156, E1

Spread across what was once a button factory, this lively bookshop and literary hub stocks both second-hand and brand-new titles in a stylish space, and puts an emphasis on local authors. (📞93 442 78 31; www.facebook.com/lacalders; Passatge de Pere Calders 9; 🕑10am-9pm Mon-Fri, 11am-9pm Sat, 11.30am-7pm Sun, closed Sun Aug; Ⓜ Poble Sec)

Brava   FASHION & ACCESSORIES

26 🔒 MAP P156, E2

Inspired by travel and the arts, fair-trade label Brava works exclusively with Catalan and other Spanish and Portuguese ateliers, and uses only sustainable materials to craft its stylishly minimalist men's and women's fashion. (www.bravafabrics.com; Carrer del Parlament 25; 🕑11am-9pm Mon-Fri, 11am-3pm & 4-9pm Sat & Sun; Ⓜ Poble Sec)

Explore

Camp Nou, Pedralbes & La Zona Alta

Some of Barcelona's most sacred sights are situated within the huge expanse stretching northwest beyond L'Eixample: the medieval monastery of Pedralbes and the great shrine to Catalan football, Camp Nou. Other reasons to venture here are Tibidabo hill, the wooded trails of the Parc Natural de Collserola, and the untouristed former towns of Sarrià and Sant Gervasi.

The Short List

○ **Camp Nou (p168)** *Reliving the great moments of legendary FC Barcelona or cheering at a live game.*

○ **Reial Monestir de Santa Maria de Pedralbes (p171)** *Wandering the 14th-century cloister and admiring exquisite medieval murals.*

○ **CosmoCaixa (p171)** *Travelling through Earth's evolution at this excellent science museum.*

○ **Bellesguard (p172)** *Gazing upon Gaudí's imposing, medieval-like masterpiece.*

○ **Tibidabo (p172)** *Escaping to this mountain for inspiring views, hiking trails and an old-fashioned amusement park.*

Getting There & Around

Ⓜ Línia 3 for Camp Nou and Palau de Pedralbes (Palau Reial).

🚆 FGC trains for Tibidabo and the Parc Natural de Collserola.

🚡 Two funicular normally run up to Tibidabo, though one was closed for renovations at research time.

Neighbourhood Map on p170

CosmoCaixa (p171) FRANTIC00/SHUTTERSTOCK ©

Top Experience 📷

Catch an FC Barcelona Game at Camp Nou

Attending a game amid the roar of the loyal crowds at the hallowed home ground of FC Barcelona is an unforgettable experience. While nothing compares to the excitement of a live match, the Barça Stadium Tour & Museum is a must for football fans; you'll get an in-depth look at the club through the multimedia museum and detailed tour.

◎ MAP P170, A6

www.fcbarcelona.com

Gate 9, Avinguda de Joan XXIII

adult/child 4-10 yr self-guided tour €29.50/23.50, guided tour €45/37

Ⓜ Palau Reial

Camp Nou Museum

Tours begin in FC Barcelona's high-tech museum, where touchscreens allow visitors to explore arcane aspects of the legendary team. Displays delve into the club's history, its social commitment and connection to Catalan identity. Sound installations include the club's anthem and the match-day roar of the crowds. A special area is devoted to Argentine Lionel Messi, considered one of the greatest footballers playing the game today.

The Stadium

Gazing out across Camp Nou is an experience in itself. The stadium, built in 1957 and enlarged for the 1982 World Cup, is one of the world's biggest, holding almost 100,000 people. After major renovations wrap up in August 2023 (the stadium will remain open throughout), Camp Nou will have a capacity of 106,000. Tours take in the visiting team's dressing room, then head out through the tunnel and on to the edge of the pitch. You'll also visit the press room. Set aside at least 1½ hours. A Players Experience ticket (adult/child €149/99) allows you to visit the FC Barcelona dressing room and includes two free photos, a virtual experience and a leaving gift.

Catching a Game

Tickets to FC Barcelona matches are available at Camp Nou, online (through FC Barcelona's official website), and through various city locations including the main Plaça de Catalunya tourist office (p182) and FC Botiga stores. Tickets can cost anything from €39 to upwards of €400. On match day, the ticket windows are open at **gate 9** (Avinguda de Joan XXIII; ⏲9.15am-7.30pm in season, 9.45am-6.30pm Mon-Sat, to 2.30pm Sun out of season, 9.15am–kick-off match days; Ⓜ Palau Reial) and gate 14 from 9.15am until kick-off. The season runs from August to May.

★ Top Tips

○ Arrive at opening time for self-guided visits to avoid the worst of the crowds, particularly during April to October.

○ You can purchase Barça Stadium Tour & Museum tickets online or from vending machines at Gate 9. No need to queue!

○ Camp Nou's **FC Botiga Megastore** (www.fcbarcelona.com; Gate 9, off Avinguda de Joan XXIII; ⏲10am-8pm, until kick-off match days; Ⓜ Palau Reial) has three floors of merchandise.

✗ Take a Break

Just inside the gates (but outside the stadium itself), you'll find star chef Carles Abellán's **Tapas 24** (☑618 478461; www.carlesabellan.com; Carrer Arístides Maillol 12; tapas €4-12; ⏲9am-9pm.

You can also grab tapas and drinks at **Lizarran** (www.lizarran.es; Carrer de Can Bruixa 6; ⏲8am-midnight; Ⓜ Les Corts), 1km northeast of Camp Nou.

Camp Nou, Pedralbes & La Zona Alta

Tibidabo ⊙ 3

⊙ 11

CosmoCaixa ⊙ 2

Ⓜ Vallcarca

 2 Peu del Funicular

Ⓜ Av Tibidabo

Av del Príncep d'Astúries

Jardins del Turó del Putget

⊙ 5 ✗

Ronda de Dalt

⊙ 4 Bellesguard

 Av de vallvdrera

C d'Iradier

Ⓜ Lesseps

Ronda de Dalt

C d'Anglí

Pg de la Bonanova

C de Mandri

C de Ganduxer

C de les Escoles Pies

C de Balmes

Av del Tibidabo

Ronda del General Mitre

Ⓐ Pàdua

Parc de Monterols

Ⓐ Ⓐ Molina

C de Muntaner

Sant Gervasi

3

Reina Elisenda 8 ✗

Parc de l'Oreneta

Plaça de Sarrià

Sarrià

Les Tres Torres

C Major de Sarrià

La Bonanova

C de Santaló

Ⓐ Muntaner

Gràcia

SARRIÀ

Via Augusta

⊙ 12

SANT GERVASI

C d'Amigó

1 ⊙ C del Bisbe Català

Reial Monestir de Santa Maria de Pedralbes

Pg de Sant Joan Bosco

Ⓐ 13

Parc del Turó

6 ⊙

Travessera de Gràcia 7 ✗

4

Av de Josep Vicenç Foix

Vil·la Amèlia Garden

Plaça de la Reina Maria Cristina

Av de Pau Casals

Plaça de Francesc Macià

C del Comte d'Urgell

C de París

PEDRALBES

Av de Pedralbes

Maria Cristina

Gran Via de Carles III

Av Diagonal

Av de Sarrià

Travessera de les Corts

C de Viladomat

Hospital Clínic

Jardins del Palau de Pedralbes

Palau Reial Ⓜ

⊙ 10

Parc de les Corts

C de Numància

C d'Entença

Av de Josep Tarradellas

Ⓜ Entença

C d'Aragó

5

ZONA UNIVERSITÀRIA

Av de Joan XXIII

LES CORTS

Ⓜ Les Corts

C de Berlin

Av de Roma

C d'Entença

Barça Stadium ⊙ Tour & Museum

Plaça del Centre

Ⓜ Sants Estació

Tarragona

C d'Aristides Maillol

Travessera de Les Corts

SANTS

Estació Sants

Parc de Joan Miró

6

Ctra de Collblanc

Av de Madrid

Badal

Plaça de Sants

Hostafrancs

C de Tarragona

Plaça d'Espanya

Ⓜ Collblanc

C de Sants

C de la Creu Coberta

Ⓜ Espanya

LA TORRASSA

For reviews see
⊙ Top Experiences p168
⊙ Sights p171
✗ Eating p173
Ⓓ Drinking p174
Ⓐ Shopping p174

0 — 500 m
0 — 0.25 miles

Sights

Reial Monestir de Santa Maria de Pedralbes MONASTERY

1 ⊙ MAP P170, A4

Founded in 1327, this serene convent is now a museum of monastic life (the few remaining nuns have moved into more modern neighbouring buildings). It stands in a residential area that was countryside until the 20th century, and which remains a divinely quiet corner of Barcelona. The convent's architectural highlight is the large, elegant, three-storey cloister, a jewel of Catalan Gothic, built in the early 14th century. The sober church is another excellent example of Catalan Gothic. (📞93 256 34 34; http://monestirpedralbes.bcn.cat;

Baixada del Monestir 9; adult/child €5/ free, from 3pm Sun & 1st Sun of month free; ⊙10am-5pm Tue-Fri, to 7pm Sat, to 8pm Sun Apr-Sep, 10am-2pm Tue-Fri, to 5pm Sat & Sun Oct-Mar; 🚍H4, V5, 63, 68, 75, 78, 🚉FGC Reina Elisenda)

CosmoCaixa MUSEUM

2 ⊙ MAP P170, B2

One of the city's most popular family-friendly attractions, this science museum is a favourite with kids (and kids at heart). The single greatest highlight is the re-creation of more than 1 sq km of flooded **Amazon rainforest** (*Bosc Inundat*). More than 100 species of Amazon flora and fauna (including anacondas, colourful poisonous frogs, and capybaras) prosper in this unique, living diorama in which you can even experience a tropical

Carrer Major de Sarrià, Sarrià (p172)

SAE JUN AHN/SHUTTERSTOCK ©

A Wander Through Old Sarrià

The old centre of elegant, affluent Sarrià is a largely pedestrianised haven of peace, with cosy squares, upmarket homes and slender streets. Founded in the 13th or 14th century and incorporated into Barcelona only in 1921, the neighbourhood unravels around sinuous, sloping Carrer Major de Sarrià, with a sprinkling of shops and restaurants. At the street's top (north) end is pretty **Plaça de Sarrià**, overlooked by the 18th-century Església de Sant Vicenç de Sarrià. Buses including 68 and V7 pass here.

As you wander downhill, duck into **Plaça del Consell de la Vila** and leafy **Plaça de Sant Vicenç de Sarrià**. Head south again to reach the 1886 **Monestir de Santa Isabel**. Around 600m further south lies the 1902 **Portal Miralles** on Passeig de Manuel Girona – a little-visited, minor Gaudí creation, this undulating wall and gateway is adorned with (faded) white *trencadís* (mosaics).

downpour. (Museu de la Ciència; 📞93 212 60 50; www.cosmocaixa.com; Carrer d'Isaac Newton 26; adult/child €6/free, guided tours from €3, planetarium €4; 🕙10am-8pm; 🚌V15, V13, 196, 123, 🚆FGC Avinguda Tibidabo)

Tibidabo   MOUNTAIN

3 ◉ MAP P170, A1

Framing the north end of the city, the pine-forested mountain of Tibidabo, which tops out at 512m, is the highest peak in Serra de Collserola. Much of its surrounding gorgeous green expanses are protected within the 80-sq-km Parc Natural de Collserola (🕙93 280 35 52; www.parcnaturalcollserola.cat; Carretera de l'Església 92), which is a delight to hike, run and cycle through.

Highlights of a trip up to Tibidabo include superb views from the top; an old-fashioned **amusement park** (📞93 211 79 42; www.tibidabo.cat; Plaça de Tibidabo 3-4; adult/child €28.50/10.30; 🕙Mar-Dec, hours vary; 👶; 🚋T2A, T2C); a **telecommunications tower** (www.torredecollserola.com; Carretera de Vallvidrera al Tibidabo; adult/child €5.60/3.30; 🕙hours vary) with viewing platform; and a looming **church** (Plaça de Tibidabo; lift €4; 🕙11am-6pm) that's visible from many parts of the city.

Bellesguard   ARCHITECTURE

4 ◉ MAP P170, B2

An entrancing work that combines Gothic and Modernista elements, this lesser-known Gaudí masterpiece was rescued from obscurity and opened to visitors in 2013. Built between 1900 and 1909, the private residence (still owned by the Guilera family) has a castle-like appearance with crenellated walls of stone and brick, narrow stained-glass windows, elaborate ironwork, gorgeous gardens and a soaring turret topped by a colourfully tiled Gaudían cross, along with spectacular city views. There's been a manor here since the 1400s. (☎93 250 40 93; www.bellesguardgaudi.com; Carrer del Bellesguard 20; adult/child 8-18 yr €9/7.20; ⏰10am-3pm Tue-Sun; ☒FGC Avinguda Tibidabo)

Eating

La Balsa   MEDITERRANEAN €€€

5 ❌ MAP P170, B2

With its grand ceiling and scented gardens surrounding a main terrace dining area, La Balsa is one of the city's premier dining addresses, founded in 1979. The seasonally changing menu mixes traditional Catalan flavours and creative expression: suckling pig with apple and cardamom, scallops with cabbage and Iberian pork loin, for example. (☎93 211 50 48; www.labalsarestaurant.com; Carrer de la Infanta Isabel 4; mains €21-28; ⏰1.30-3.15pm & 8.30-10.30pm; ☏; ☒FGC Avinguda Tibidabo)

Aspic   CAFE €€

6 ❌ MAP P170, C4

At the flagship cafe of this Barcelona caterer, luxury ingredients – smoked salmon, premium charcuterie and cheeses, high-grade olive oils, carefully chosen Spanish wines – step into the spotlight in stunning seasonal soups, creative market-based salads and dishes like wild sea bass with garlic. The attached deli is perfect for picking up a gourmet picnic to eat in nearby Parc del Turó. (☎93 200 04 35; www.aspic.es; Avinguda de Pau Casals 24; dishes €10-20; ⏰9am-midnight Tue-Sat, to 4pm Sun; ☏☒; ☒T1, T2, T3 Francesc Macià)

Tapas 24   TAPAS €

7 ❌ MAP P170, D4

Barcelona's favourite chef Carles Abellán brings his signature up-market twist on classic tapas to this neon-lit corner cafe. Top picks are the sensational *bikini* toastie (made with truffle and cured ham), just-cooked tortilla, lemon-marinated anchovies and creamy Andalucian *payoyo* cheese. No bookings. (☎93 858 93 29; www.carlesabellan.com; Avinguda Diagonal 520; tapas €4-12; ⏰7.45am-midnight Mon-Fri, from 9am Sat & Sun; Ⓜ Diagonal)

Vivanda   CATALAN €€

8 ❌ MAP P170, A3

Diners are in for a treat with the knockout menu conceived by acclaimed Catalan chef Jordi Vilà. Delicate tapas and *platillos* (sharing plates) showcase the freshest seasonal fare, from artisan cheeses to vegetable ravioli and oven-baked wild fish with potatoes. Hidden behind a reincarnated Sarrià home, the tree-shaded terrace has winter heat lamps, blankets and broths. (☎93 203 19 18; www.vivanda.cat; Carrer Major de Sarrià 134; tapas €4-14, sharing plates €10-22; ⏰1.30-3.30pm & 8.30-11pm Tue-Sat, 1.30-3.30pm Sun; ☒; ☒FGC Reina Elisenda)

Cerveceria Casa Fernández

SPANISH €€

9 ✗ MAP P170, D4

The family team behind gracefully old-school L'Eixample bar Dry Martini (p127) is in charge at this smart, lively, long-running spot decorated with local artwork. With tables on the pavement or inside amid hot-red walls and jazzy murals, its ideal for elegantly yet unfussily pre-pared Catalan cuisine – Padrón peppers, L'Escala anchovies, *patates braves*, fried eggs with home-cooked chips – and creative international bites. (Casa Fernández; ☎93 201 93 08; www.drymartiniorg.com; Carrer de San-taló 46; tapas €4-12, mains €9-20; ⏰1-5pm & 8pm-midnight Mon-Sat, noon-midnight Sun; ☒FGC Gràcia)

Drinking

El Maravillas

COCKTAIL BAR

10 ☻ MAP P170, B5

Overlooking Les Corts' peace-ful Plaça de la Concòrdia, El Maravillas is an escape from the crowded Ciutat Vella (Old City). Andreu Estríngana, one of Spain's top mixologists, and team concoct creative cocktails (€7 to €12) named for celebrated sports players. Spanish wines and easy-drinking vermouths are other drinks of choice. (☎93 360 73 78; www.elmaravillas.cat; Plaça de la Concòrdia 15; ⏰noon-midnight Sun-Tue, to 1am Wed, to 2am Thu, to

3am Fri & Sat; Ⓜ Les Corts, ☒T1, T2, T3 Numància)

Gimlet

COCKTAIL BAR

Under the watch of the talented folk behind popular restaurant Cerveceria Casa Fernández next door (see 9 ✗ Map p170, D4), stylishly updated Gimlet is one of Barce-lona's oldest cocktail bars. Dry martinis and, of course, gimlets are the signature drinks. There are also cocktail-making workshops. (☎93 201 53 06; www.drymartiniorg. com; Carrer de Santaló 46; ⏰6pm-1am Mon-Wed, to 2.30am Thu, to 3am Fri & Sat; ☒T1, T2, T3 Francesc Macià, ☒FGC Muntaner)

Mirablau

BAR

11 ☻ MAP P170, C1

Views over the entire city from this balcony bar, restaurant and club at the base of the Funicular del Tibidabo make up for some-times patchy service. The bar is renowned for its impressive gin selection (€12 to €15). (☎93 418 58 79; www.mirablaubcn.com; Plaça del Doctor Andreu; ⏰11am-3.30am Mon-Wed, to 4.30am Thu, 10am-5am Fri & Sat, 10am-2.30am Sun; ☒196, ☒FGC Avinguda Tibidabo)

Shopping

Mercat de Galvany

MARKET

12 🔒 MAP P170, D4

Opened in 1927, Galvany is one of the city's most beautiful markets, with a brick facade and glass- and cast-iron interior. Over 80 stalls sell an enticing variety of bakery items, fresh produce and deli goods, and there's also a low-key cafe. (www.mercatgalvany.es; Carrer de Santaló 65; ☉7am-2.30pm Mon-Thu & Sat year-round, to 8pm Fri approx Sep-May; ⊞FGC Muntaner)

Catalina House

HOMEWARES

13 🔒 MAP P170, D4

After its decade-long success on the Balearic island of Formentera, Catalina House now has a second branch in Barcelona's Sant Gervasi. Sustainable materials such as linen, cotton, stone, glass, terracotta and oil-treated recycled timbers are used in stylish Mediterranean designs for the home. (🖉93 140 96 39; www.catalinahouse.net; Carrer d'Amigó 47; ☉10.15am-2pm & 5-8pm Mon-Fri, 10.30am-2pm Sat; ⊞FGC Muntaner)

Bikini preparation at Tapas 24 (p173)

Survival Guide

Before You Go

Book Your Stay

○ Wherever (and whenever) you stay, it's wise to book well ahead.

○ Staying in the Barri Gòtic, El Raval or La Ribera puts you in the heart of the action, but nights can be noisy from Thursday to Sunday.

○ L'Eixample can be quieter (assuming you're not on a busy boulevard), while Barceloneta and El Poblenou are perfect for the beach.

○ Outer neighbourhoods mean more transport, but a quieter escape and often fabulous views.

Useful Websites

Booking.com and, controversially, Airbnb (due to its alleged impact on rental prices for locals and on neighbourhood character), are of course popular accommodation-booking portals. Other options:

Aparteasy (www. aparteasy.com)

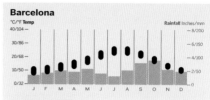

Barcelona

°C/°F Temp / Rainfall Inches/mm

When to Go

○ **Summer (Jun–Aug)** Hot beach weather, but often overwhelmed with visitors in July and August; locals escape in August.

○ **Autumn (Sep–Nov)** September is one of the best months to visit (including the Festes de la Mercé); October and November are quieter and cooler.

○ **Winter (Dec–Feb)** Nights can be chilly and there's a chance of rain, but there are fewer visitors and sunny days are possible.

○ **Spring (Mar–May)** A lovely time to visit. Manageable visitor numbers; mixed weather.

Rent the Sun (www. rentthesun.com)

Barcelona On Line (www.barcelona-on-line.com)

Friendly Rentals (www. friendlyrentals.com)

MH Apartments (www. mhapartments.com)

Apartment Barcelona (www.apartmentbarcelona.com)

Idealista (www.idealista.com)

Lonely Planet (www. lonelyplanet.com/spain/barcelona/hotels)

Best Budget

Casa Gràcia (www. casagraciabcn.com) Stylish, social hostel with white-and-gold rooms.

360 Hostel Arts & Culture (www.360hostelarts. com) Buzzy scene in an art-filled design hostel.

Pensió 2000 (www. pensio2000.com) Family-run guesthouse overlooking the Palau de la Música Catalana.

Pars Tailor's Hostel (www.parshostels.

com) Budget-chic Sant Antoni choice with vintage vibe.

TOC Hostel (www.tochostels.com) Modern dorms, private rooms, fab dip pool; in L'Eixample.

Best Midrange

Praktik Rambla (www.hotelpraktikrambla.com) A 19th-century L'Eixample mansion turned boutique beauty.

Hotel Brummell (www.hotelbrummell.com) Boutique bliss (pool, cafe, yoga) in Poble Sec.

Five Rooms (www.thefiverooms.com) Charming L'Eixample pick with designer rooms.

Casa Mathilda (www.casamathilda.com) Intimate, styled-up 1920s building in northern L'Eixample.

Best Top End

El Palace (www.hotelpalacebarcelona.com) A plushly updated grand dame of L'Eixample.

Casa Bonay (www.casabonay.com) Designer Catalan-inspired interiors in an 1896 L'Eixample building.

Hotel Neri (www.hotelneri.com) Beautiful, historical hotel in the thick of the Barri Gòtic.

The Serras (www.hotheserrasbarcelona.com) Sleek portside five-star; rooftop pool.

Arriving in Barcelona

Aeroport de Barcelona–El Prat

The **Aeroport de Barcelona–El Prat** (☑ 91 321 10 00; www.aena.es; 🐛) lies 15km southwest of Plaça de Catalunya at El Prat de Llobregat.

Bus The **A1 Aerobús** (☑ 902 100104; www.aerobusbcn.com; Plaça d'Espanya; one way/return €5.90/10.20; ⏱ 5.05am-12.35am; Ⓜ Espanya) runs from T1 to Plaça de Catalunya (30 to 40 minutes) via Plaça d'Espanya, Gran Via de les Corts Catalanes (corner of Carrer del Comte d'Urgell) and Plaça de la Universitat every five to 10 minutes from 5.35am to 1.05am. Buses from Plaça de Catalunya to

the airport run every five to 10 minutes from 5am to 12.30am, stopping at the corner of Carrer de Sepúlveda and Carrer del Comte d'Urgell, and at Plaça d'Espanya. The **A2 Aerobús** from T2 to Plaça de Catalunya runs from 5.35am to 1am every 10 minutes, following the same route as the A1 Aerobús. Fares on both are €5.90/10.20 single/return.

Metro *Línia* 9 Sud (L9S) connects T1 and T2 with Zona Universitària (32 minutes) every seven minutes 5am to midnight Sunday to Thursday, 5am to 2am on Friday and 24 hours on Sunday; change lines en route for Barcelona city centre (€5.15).

Taxi Costs €25 to €35 to/from centre (30 minutes).

Train From 5.42am to 11.38pm, Renfe (www.renfe.com) runs the half-hourly R2 Nord train line from the airport via several stops to Barcelona's main train station, Estació Sants (20 minutes) and Passeig de Gràcia (27 minutes). The first service for the airport from Passeig de Gràcia leaves at 5.08am and the last at 11.06pm; all pass through Estació Sants around five minutes later. One-way tickets cost €4.20. The airport train station is a five-minute walk from T2. Free 24-hour shuttle buses (10 to 20 minutes) link the train station and T2 with T1 every five to 15 minutes.

Estació Sants

○ Barcelona's main train station is Sants, 2.5km west of La Rambla.

○ Train is the most convenient overland option for reaching Barcelona from major Spanish centres like Madrid and Valencia. The high-speed TGV train takes around 6½ hours to/from Paris.

○ A network of *rodalies/cercanías* run by Renfe (www.renfe.com) serves towns around Barcelona (and the airport).

Estació d'Autobusos Barcelona Nord

○ Barcelona's long-haul **bus station** (Estació del Nord; 93 706 53 66; www. barcelonanord.cat; Carrer d'Alí Bei 80; M Arc de Triomf) is in L'Eixample, a short walk from the Arc de Triomf metro station. Buses

fan out across Spain, many under **Alsa** (902 422242; www.alsa.es).

○ **Eurolines** (www. eurolines.es) is the main international bus carrier, serving Europe and Morocco from the Estació del Nord and the **Estació d'Autobusos de Sants** (Carrer de Viriat; M Sants Estació).

Aeroport de Girona–Costa Brava

○ **Girona-Costa Brava airport** (www.aena.es), 13km southwest of Girona and 92km northeast of Barcelona, is served by flights from across Europe.

○ The **Sagalés Airport Line** (902 130014; www. sagalesairportline.com; one way/return €16/25; M Arc de Triomf) runs between Girona–Costa Brava airport and Barcelona's Estació del Nord bus station (€16, 1¼ hours, three to four daily).

Aeroport de Reus

Reus airport (91 321 10 00; www.aena.es), 13km west of Tarragona and 108km southwest of Barcelona, has flights from across Europe.

Hispano-Igualadina (93 339 73 29; www. igualadina.com; Carrer de Viriat; M Sants Estació) links Reus airport with Barcelona's Estació d'Autobusos de Sants (€16, 1¾ hours).

Getting Around

Metro

○ The easy-to-use **Transports Metropolitans de Barcelona (TMB)** metro system (www.tmb.cat) has 11 numbered and colour-coded lines. It runs 5am to midnight Sunday to Thursday, to 2am on Friday and 24 hours on Saturday.

○ The metro, FGC trains, *rodalies/cercanías* (Renfe-run local trains) and buses come under a combined system. Targeta T-Casual (10-ride passes; €11.35) are the best value; otherwise, it's €2.40 per ride in Zone 1.

Bus

○ **Transports Metropolitans de Barcelona** (www.tmb.cat) buses run along most city routes every few minutes from between 5am and 6.30am to around 10pm or 11pm. Many routes pass through Plaça de Catalunya and/or Plaça de la Universitat.

o After 11pm, **Nitbus** (www.ambmobilitat.cat) runs a reduced network of 17 yellow night buses until 3am or 5am (including N17 to/from the airport). Almost all *nitbus* routes pass through Plaça de Catalunya and most run every 30 to 45 minutes.

Taxi

Taxis charge €2.25 flag fall plus meter charges of €1.18 per kilometre (€1.41 from 8pm to 8am and all day on weekends). A further €4.30 is added for all trips to/from the airport and €2.50/€4.30 for

journeys starting from Estació Sants/the port. You can flag a taxi down, call one or book through a wealth of app- and/or website-based companies.

Train

o Suburban trains run by the **Ferrocarrils de la Generalitat de Catalunya** (FGC; www.fgc.net) include useful city lines. All lines heading north from Plaça de Catalunya stop at Carrer de Provença and Gràcia; L7 goes to near Tibidabo and L6 goes to Reina Elisenda, near the Monestir de Pedralbes.

o FGC trains run from about 5am (with only one or two services before 6am) to 11pm or midnight Sunday to Thursday, and from 5am to about 1am on Friday and Saturday.

Bicycle

o Barcelona has more than 180km of bike lanes.

o Bike-hire outlets are everywhere, particularly in the Barri Gòtic, El Raval and La Ribera; from €5 per hour.

o Barcelona's main bike-share scheme **Bicing** (www.bicing.barcelona) is, for now, geared towards residents rather than tourists.

Cable Car

Telefèric del Port (p161) Travels between the waterfront southwest of Barceloneta and Montjuïc.

Telefèric de Montjuïc (p161) Runs between Parc Montjuïc and the Castell de Montjuïc.

Dos & Don'ts

Greetings Catalans, like other Spaniards, often greet friends and strangers alike with a kiss on both cheeks, although two males rarely do this.

Eating and drinking In more casual restaurants and bars, keep your cutlery between courses.

Visiting churches It is considered disrespectful to visit churches as a tourist during Mass and other worship services. Taking photos at such times is a definite no-no, as is visiting without dressing appropriately.

Escalators Stand on the right to let people pass, especially on the metro.

Essential Information

Accessible Travel

○ All buses in Barcelona are wheelchair accessible, as are most metro stations (generally by lift; check www.tmb.cat/en/transport-accessible), hotels, street crossings and public institutions.

○ Ticket vending machines in metro stations are adapted for travellers with disabilities and have Braille options.

○ **Barcelona Turisme** (☎93 285 38 34; www.barcelonaturisme.com; Plaça de Catalunya 17-S, underground; ⏱8.30am-9pm; Ⓜ Catalunya) provides details of accessible hotels and runs a wheelchair-accessible tour of the Barri Gòtic (€13.95).

○ Several taxi companies have adapted vehicles, including **Taxi Amic** (☎93 420 80 88; www.taxi-amic-adaptat.com) and **Greentaxi** (☎900 827900; www.greentaxi.es).

○ From July to mid-September and on weekends in June, volunteers at several beaches provide amphibious chairs and assistance.

Business Hours

Restaurants 1pm–4pm and 8.30pm–midnight; some open all day

Shops 9am or 10am–1.30pm or 2pm and 4pm or 4.30pm–8pm or 8.30pm Monday to Saturday

Bars 6pm–2am (to 3am weekends)

Clubs Midnight–6am Thursday to Saturday

Banks 8.30am–2pm Monday to Friday; some also 4pm–7pm Thursday or 9am–1pm Saturday

Discount Cards

Articket BCN (www.articketbcn.org) Admission to six major art galleries for €35.

Arqueoticket (www.barcelonaturisme.com) Admission to four major history and archaeology galleries for €14.50.

Barcelona Card (www.barcelonacard.com) Costs €20/46/56/61 for two/three/four/five days; free transport and discounted or free sights admission.

Ruta del Modernisme (www.rutadelmodernisme.com) Modernista sights at discounted rates; costs €12.

Electricity

Type C
230V/50Hz

Emergencies

Ambulance	☎061
EU standard emergency number	☎112
Country code	☎34
International access code	☎00
Guàrdia Urbana	☎092

Public Holidays

New Year's Day (Any Nou/Año Nuevo)
1 January

Epiphany/Three Kings' Day (Epifanía or El Dia dels Reis/Día de los Reyes Magos) 6 January

Good Friday (Divendres Sant/Viernes Santo) March/April

Easter Monday (Dilluns de Pasqua Florida/Lunes de Pascua) March/April

Labour Day (Dia del Treball/Fiesta del Trabajo) 1 May

Day after Pentecost Sunday (Dilluns de Pasqua Granada) May/June

Feast of St John the Baptist (Dia de Sant Joan/Día de San Juan Bautista) 24 June

Feast of the Assumption (L'Assumpció/La Asunción) 15 August

Catalonia's National Day (Diada Nacional de Catalunya) 11 September

Festes de la Mercè 24 September

Spanish National Day (Festa de la Hispanitat/Día de la Hispanidad) 12 October

All Saints Day (Dia de Tots Sants/Día de Todos los Santos) 1 November

Constitution Day (Dia de la Constitució/Día de la Constitución) 6 December

Feast of the Immaculate Conception (La Immaculada Concepció/La Inmaculada Concepción) 8 December

Christmas (Nadal/Navidad) 25 December

Boxing Day/St Stephen's Day (Dia de Sant Esteve) 26 December

Telephone

○ You can buy local SIM cards and prepaid data and call time in Spain for your own mobile phone (provided you own an unlocked phone that is compatible – these days most are compatible, though the Japanese system may not be).

○ Travellers with phones from within the EU have free roaming.

Tourist Information

Plaça de Catalunya (☑ 93 285 38 34; www.barcelonaturisme.com; Plaça de Catalunya 17-S, underground; ⏱ 8.30am-9pm; Ⓜ Catalunya)

Plaça Sant Jaume (☑ 93 285 38 34; www.barcelonaturisme.com; Plaça de Sant Jaume; ⏱ 8.30am-8pm Mon-Fri, 9am-3pm Sat & Sun; Ⓜ Catalunya)

Catedral (☑ 93 368 97 00; www.barcelonaturisme.com; Plaça Nova, Col·legi d'Arquitectes; ⏱ 9am-7pm Mon-Sat, to 3pm Sun)

Estació Sants (☑ 93 285 38 34; www.barcelonaturisme.com; Barcelona Sants; ⏱ 8.30am-8.30pm daily Apr-Oct, 8.30am-8.30pm Mon-Fri, to 2.30pm Sat & Sun Nov-Mar; Ⓡ Sants Estació)

Aeroport del Prat (☑ 93 285 38 32; www.

Tipping

Restaurants Catalans typically leave 5% or less at restaurants. Leave more for exceptionally good service.

Taxis Optional, but most locals round up to the nearest euro.

Bars It's rare to tip in bars, though small change is appreciated.

Warning: Watch Your Belongings

○ Petty crime (bag-snatching, pickpocketing) is a major problem, especially in the touristed city centre. You're especially vulnerable when dragging luggage to/from hotels; know your route.

○ Avoid walking around El Raval and the southern end of La Rambla late at night.

○ Take nothing of value to the beach and don't leave anything unattended.

barcelonaturisme.com; Aeroport de Barcelona– El Prat, Terminal 2; ⏱ 8.30am-8.30pm)

Visas

Citizens or residents of EU & Schengen countries No visa required.

Citizens or residents of UK, Australia, Canada, Israel, Japan, New Zealand, the USA and most Latin American countries From 2022, nationals of these countries will require prior authorisation to enter Spain under the new European Travel Information and Authorisation System (ETIAS; www.etias.com). With ETIAS pre-authorisation, travellers can stay in Spain visa-free for 90 days within any given 180-day period.

Other countries Check with a Spanish embassy or consulate.

Responsible Travel

Overtourism

○ Travel off-season (outside May to September and Easter), and mid-week.

○ Tourist apartments and illegal lets are driving up rents for locals. Stay in official registered accommodation (www. fairtourism.barcelona).

○ Combine your trip with exploring other parts of Catalonia: Girona, Roman Tarragona, the Pyrenees.

○ Read up on sustainable tourism projects and responsible travel

tips (https://meet. barcelona.cat).

Support Local & Give Back

○ Join a volunteering project (https://www. barcelona.cat/en/get involved) and/or beach clean-up (https://clean beachinitiative.org).

○ Enjoy a guided tour to support local experts. **Hidden City Tours** (www. hiddencitytours.com) works with guides who have been part of the city's homeless community.

○ Rising rents have closed some traditional shops; shop at long-established favourites with special preservation status (p57).

○ Support hospitality-training programmes for those struggling to access the job market (including undocumented migrants) at Espai Mescladís (p88).

Leave a Light Footprint

Bike-share scheme Bicing isn't aimed at tourists, but there are plenty of bike-rental operators such as **Bike Tours Barcelona** (www. biketoursbarcelona.com).

Language

Both Spanish (known as *castellano*, or Castilian) and Catalan (*català*, spoken in Catalonia) are official languages in Spain. Eivissenc is the native dialect of Catalan spoken on Ibiza and Formentera. You'll be perfectly well understood speaking Spanish in Ibiza and you'll find that most locals will happily speak Spanish to you, especially once they realise you're a foreigner. Here we've provided you with some Spanish to get you started, as well as some Catalan basics at the end.

Just read our pronunciation guides as if they were English and you'll be understood. Note that (m/f) indicates masculine and feminine forms.

To enhance your trip with a phrasebook, visit **lonelyplanet.com**.

Basics

Hello.
Hola.   o·la

Goodbye.
Adiós.   a·dyos

How are you?
¿Qué tal?   ke tal

Fine, thanks.
Bien, gracias.   byen gra·thyas

Please.
Por favor.   por fa·vor

Thank you.
Gracias.   gra·thyas

Excuse me.
Perdón.   per·don

Sorry.
Lo siento.   lo syen·to

Yes./No.
Sí./No.   see/no

Do you speak (English)?
¿Habla (inglés)?   a·bla (een·gles)

I (don't) understand.
Yo (no) entiendo. yo (no) en·tyen·do

Eating & Drinking

I'm a vegetarian. (m/f)
Soy   soy
vegetariano/a.   ve·khe·ta·rya·no/a

Cheers!
¡Salud!   sa·loo

That was delicious!
¡Estaba   es·ta·ba
buenísimo!   bwe·nee·see·mo

Please bring the bill.
Por favor nos   por fa·vor nos
trae la cuenta.   tra·e la kwen·ta

I'd like ...
Quisiera ...   kee·sye·ra ...

a coffee   *un café*   oon ka·fe

a table   *una mesa*   oo·na me·sa
  for two   *para dos*   pa·ra dos

a wine   *un vino*   oon vee·no

two beers   *dos*   dos
                cervezas   ther·ve·thas

Shopping

I'd like to buy ...
Quisiera   kee·sye·ra
comprar ...   kom·prar ...

May I look at it?
¿Puedo verlo?   pwe·do ver·lo

How much is it?
¿Cuánto cuesta?   kwan·to kwes·ta

That's too/very expensive.
Es muy caro.   es mooy ka·ro

Emergencies

Help!
¡Socorro!   so·ko·ro

Call a doctor!
¡Llame a oon   lya·me a oon
un médico!   me·dee·ko

Call the police!
¡Llame a   lya·me a
la policía!   la po·lee·thee·a

I'm lost. (m/f)
Estoy perdido/a.   es·toy per·dee·do/a

I'm ill. (m/f)
Estoy enfermo/a.   es·toy en·fer·mo/a

Where are the toilets?
¿Dónde están   don·de es·tan
los baños?   los ba·nyos

Time & Numbers

What time is it?
¿Qué hora es?   ke o·ra es

It's (10) o'clock.
Son (las diez).   son (las dyeth)

morning	mañana	ma·nya·na
afternoon	tarde	tar·de
evening	noche	no·che
yesterday	ayer	a·yer
today	hoy	oy
tomorrow	mañana	ma·nya·na

1	uno	oo·no
2	dos	dos
3	tres	tres
4	cuatro	kwa·tro
5	cinco	theen·ko
6	seis	seys
7	siete	sye·te
8	ocho	o·cho
9	nueve	nwe·ve
10	diez	dyeth

Transport & Directions

Where's ...?
¿Dónde está ...?   don·de es·ta ...

What's the address?
¿Cuál es la   kwal es la
dirección?   dee·rek·thyon

Can you show me (on the map)?
¿Me lo puede   me lo pwe·de
indicar   een·dee·kar
(en el mapa)?   (en el ma·pa)

I want to go to ...
Quisiera ir a ...   kee·sye·ra eer a ...

What time does it arrive/leave?
¿A qué hora   a ke o·ra
llega/sale?   lye·ga/sa·le

I want to get off here.
Quiero bajarme   kye·ro ba·khar·me
aquí.   a·kee

Catalan – Basics

Good morning.
Bon dia.   bon dee·a

Good afternoon.
Bona tarda.   bo·na tar·da

Good evening.
Bon vespre.   bon bes·pra

Goodbye.
Adéu.   a·the·oo

Please.
Sisplau.   sees·pla·oo

Thank you.
Gràcies.   gra·see·a

You're welcome.
De res.   de res

Excuse me.
Perdoni.   par·tho·nee

I'm sorry.
Ho sento.   oo sen·to

How are you?
Com estàs?   kom as·tas

Very well.
(Molt) Bé.   (mol) be

Behind the Scenes

Send Us Your Feedback

We love to hear from travellers – your comments help make our books better. We read every word, and we guarantee that your feedback goes straight to the authors. Visit **lonelyplanet.com/contact** to submit your updates and suggestions.

Note: We may edit, reproduce and incorporate your comments in Lonely Planet products such as guidebooks, websites and digital products, so let us know if you don't want your comments reproduced or your name acknowledged. For a copy of our privacy policy visit lonelyplanet.com/privacy.

Isabella's Thanks

An enormous *gràcies* to everyone who helped out on all things Barcelona: Sally Davies, Esme Fox, Marwa El-Hennawey Preston, Tom Stainer, the Devour team, Clementina Milà, Joan Pau Aragón, María del Río, Vera de Frutos, Suzy Taher, Isabelle Kliger, Nigel Haywood, Alex Pérez, Lorna Turnbull, José Fabra and friends, Pau Gavaldà, David Doyes, and Ariadna and family. As always, the biggest thanks (and *salut!*) to my loyal research assistants Jack Noble, John Noble and Andrew Brannan.

Acknowledgements

Cover photographs: City view from from Park Güell, Georgios Tsichlis/ Shutterstock ©; Popular souvenir, Iakov Filimonov/Shutterstock © Photographs pp 32–3 (clockwise from top left): doble-d/Getty Images ©; David J. Lew/500px ©; alionabirukova/Shutterstock ©; GypsyPictureShow/Shutterstock ©

This Book

This 7th edition of Lonely Planet's *Pocket Barcelona* guidebook was researched and written by Isabella Noble. The previous edition was written by Sally Davies and Catherine Le Nevez and the 5th edition was written by Regis St Louis and Sally Davies.

This guidebook was produced by the following:

Senior Product Editors Sandie Kestell, Jess Ryan

Product Editors Kate Kiely, Angela Tinson

Cartographers Hunor Csutoros, Valentina Kremenchutskaya, Anthony Phelan

Book Designers Catalina Aragón, Fergal Condon,

Katherine Marsh

Assisting Editors William Allen, Andrea Dobbin, Carly Hall, Lorna Parkes, Rachel Rawling

Cover Researcher Brendan Dempsey-Spencer

Thanks to Hannah Cartmel, Joel Cotterell, Karen Henderson, Sonia Kapoor, Darren O'Connell, Genna Patterson, Thy Riedel

Index

See also separate subindexes for:

⊗ **Eating p190**

◌ **Drinking p191**

✪ **Entertainment p191**

⊕ **Shopping p191**

Index